Attention Is the New Currency

Praise for *Attention Is the New Currency*

"As a creator who has spent years building an online platform, I appreciate how honest and practical this book is. *Attention Is the New Currency* breaks down what it really takes to turn attention into a meaningful and sustainable career. This guide gives creators a clear and practical road map for building something authentic and lasting."

—Jessii Vee (@JessiiVee)

"This isn't just for aspiring influencers—it's a modern guide for anyone trying to find their online community, regardless of whether that's for a side hustle, nonprofit, social movement, or passion project. This is for people who are ready to reach out and make social media their tool for positive impact."

—Lawrence Dalusung, influencer marketing professional

"In a world that runs on social media, Marissa and Shanna make it simple to learn how to break through the complex industry to make a name for yourself!"

—Melissa Tierney (@MissyonMadison)

"Anyone working in or hoping to work in online marketing or content creation should read this book. *Attention Is the New Currency* cuts through the noise and shares practical, proven strategies for building an audience. Imagine if I'd had this book when I first started out! How nice that would have been!"

—Nina Nelson (@NinaNelson), coauthor of *The Clear Skin Diet*

"WOW, I am hooked! *Attention is the New Currency* is the perfect guide for anyone who wants a long-term career in social media. It's real, actionable, and inspiring—Marissa Rachel and Shanna Lisa are the relatable influencers everyone should learn from!"

—Estrella Serrato (@CafecitoconEstrellita),
podcast host and founder of Cafecito con Estrellita

"*Attention Is the New Currency* is a helpful and motivating tool for existing and aspiring content creators alike. It offers practical, actionable advice on how to find your authentic voice and use it to capture an audience's attention. The book pulls back the curtain on what it takes to grow and guide your social media platforms with intention and impact."

—Kelleth Cuthbert (@KellethCuthbert), actress and model

"I wish this book existed when I started. *Attention Is the New Currency* tells the truth about growth, money, boundaries, and burnout—while actually showing you how to build a platform that still feels like you."

—Randa Nelson (@RandaNelson), Netflix producer
and coauthor of *The Clear Skin Diet*

Attention Is the New Currency

The Ultimate Guide to **Standing Out** and **Getting Paid** on Social Media

Marissa Rachel and Shanna Lisa

BENBELLA

BenBella Books, Inc.
Dallas, TX

BENBELLA

BenBella Books, Inc.
8080 N. Central Expressway
Suite 1700
Dallas, TX 75206
benbellabooks.com
Send feedback to feedback@benbellabooks.com

BenBella is a federally registered trademark.

Printed in the United States of America
10 9 8 7 6 5 4 3 2 1

Library of Congress Control Number: 2026009153
ISBN 9781637748800 (trade paperback)
ISBN 9781637748817 (electronic)

Editing by Victoria Carmody
Copyediting by Elizabeth Degenhard
Proofreading by Martha Gallant
Indexing by WordCo Indexing Services
Text design and composition by PerfecType, Nashville, TN
Author photo by Jessica Gray
Cover design by Sarah Avinger
Cover image © Adobe Stock / Natalia S
Printed by Lake Book Manufacturing

For you, the one who's been waiting for the right moment. This is it.

Contents

Introduction

Hey there! Welcome to the wild, weird world of social media! We're so glad you decided to pick up this book!

Becoming a social media creator is a deeply personal and often unpredictable journey. No two creators start from the same place, and no two paths look the same.

Your path is yours alone. The reasons that led you here, the dreams that drive you, and the content you create are entirely your own. You're not really competing with anyone else. It might feel that way sometimes, especially when you see someone else blow up overnight. But the reality is, your only real competition is yourself. Your story, your voice, and your perspective are what make your content valuable.

We've had our own journey, filled with lessons, challenges, and breakthroughs. While our experience won't mirror yours, we're here to share what we've learned from our own experience (the mistakes, the wins, and the unexpected lessons) in hopes that it helps you along the way and empowers you to carve your own path.

We're not here to give you vague advice about "chasing your dreams" or "working hard." We want to get practical. You'll learn how to set realistic goals, create content you're genuinely proud of, and build a routine that keeps you consistent without burning yourself out. We'll also get into the tough stuff, like what to do when your growth stalls, how to handle negative comments, and how to set boundaries so social media doesn't take over your life.

And of course, we'll talk about money. Because if you're putting in the work, you should absolutely know how to turn your platform into income.

Everyone can leverage content to broaden their opportunities. Attention is the new currency, and the power of a well-crafted online presence cannot be overstated. A coveted blue checkmark, a substantial follower count, and a meticulously curated digital persona can add credibility across diverse fields such as fitness, politics, medicine, parenthood, journalism, acting, and writing, to name a few. The potential to attract new customers and opportunities is undeniable.

The difference between a "regular person" and a "social media star" isn't magic; it's strategy. (And maybe a ring light!) By the time you finish this book, you won't just feel inspired, you'll have a clear plan of action to turn your social media dreams into reality—something doable, sustainable, and aligned with who you are.

So, Who Is Marissa Rachel?

We're Marissa and Shanna. Professionally, we go by Marissa Rachel and Shanna Lisa, but you can call us Marissa and Shanna, because we're cool with you like that. We're sisters—Shanna is older by four years, but Marissa is taller by four inches, so it all evens out.

We've been in the social media game a long, looooong time! We started our YouTube channel in 2012, but we were creating content for an online audience even earlier than that. Shanna started her first blog back in 2007, which documented her travels living abroad in Paris, Germany, the Caribbean, and Australia. She also started a short-lived fashion blog in 2010. But it wasn't until we joined forces and activated our powerful sister energy that we decided to start our Marissa Rachel YouTube channel.

We both put in equal work when we built our channel, so you might wonder why the channel is called "Marissa Rachel." Well, when we started out, Shanna was on one of her many international adventures and living in Sydney, Australia, so Marissa was filming videos by herself for a while. And then, we just stuck with the name! Once we content creators are professionally known as a particular name, we're reluctant to change it because of how it will affect search engine optimization (SEO). Since then, we've grown our YouTube channel to more than 1 million followers and our overall social media following to more than 2 million. But more importantly, we've accomplished some of our wildest dreams along the way! We've given a TEDx talk, spoken at the United Nations General Assembly (twice!), and been featured in *Forbes* four times. We've flown on private planes, met legendary rock stars, visited movie sets, gone backstage at concerts, and walked countless red carpets. We've gotten free VIP trips to places like Walt Disney World and the Coachella music festival. We've earned enough money to buy our dream home in Los Angeles. And we've been able to give back, donating tens of thousands of pads and tampons to female veterans through the American Red Cross, and encouraging people to adopt homeless cats and dogs with the Best Friends Animal Society.

This journey has been a rollercoaster full of highs, lows, and a few "what the hell are we doing?" moments. Now, we're handing over everything we've learned so you can skip some of the chaos and carve out your own path to success (preferably with fewer facepalm moments than we had).

Helping You Carve Out Your Path

We're not here to promise overnight fame. But if you're willing to treat this like a real job, with strategy, intention, and consistency, you can absolutely turn social media into a career.

This book won't just help you get inspired or dream big. It'll also show you how to actually build something that works. There is a method to finding success on social media. We didn't blow up overnight. We didn't have some special "it factor" or magnetic personality that made people gravitate toward us. We didn't just get lucky. We got strategic. We studied what worked, experimented, failed a lot, and then started being more intentional about our content. Once we did that, things began to click. It's not random, and it's not magic. You don't need to burn yourself out, sell your soul, or sit around waiting for a post to go viral. Our success was calculated, built from trial and error, smart strategy, and learning how to play the game. If something can be calculated, it can be replicated. And if we did it, so can you.

PART 1

Getting Set Up

1

Finding Your Direction

So you want to be a social media star? Or maybe you just want to level up your personal account and share better content with friends. Maybe you want to explore ways to make money with your existing accounts. Maybe you're just curious about how the influencers you keep hearing about built their channels. Regardless of what brought you here, we're happy you're starting your journey, and Shanna Lisa and Marissa Rachel are here to guide you every step of the way!

In this chapter, we walk you through the very first steps to becoming a content creator. Too many creators chase vague goals like "getting big" and end up burned out or directionless. Before you can jump right into creating content, it's important to identify what you actually want to achieve by using social media. Take time to define what success means to you, whether it's building a career, landing brand deals, selling products, promoting a cause, or creating a platform that opens doors.

Once your goals and definition of success are clear, start creating and see what resonates. You can always adjust as you go. Stay flexible, stay authentic, and make content you genuinely enjoy. That combination of clarity, purpose, and adaptability is the foundation for building a sustainable and fulfilling social media career.

Setting Your Goals

Okay, real talk! One of the biggest mistakes we made when we started was thinking that the goal was to just . . . get big. More followers, more views, more attention. That's what we thought success looked like. We thought if we could just rack up numbers, we'd "make it." And truthfully? That's why we floundered for a while. Because we had zero clue what we actually wanted beyond vague internet fame.

So before you go any further, do yourself a favor and figure out what you actually want to get out of your social presence. Like, right now. Grab a pen and write it down. What are your goals? Is it to get free PR packages, land brand deals, or make money? Do you want to quit your nine-to-five and build a full-time influencer career? Are you looking to establish yourself as an expert in your field? Or do you just want a creative outlet and a place to express yourself? Be honest—no filter.

And listen, if your goal is purely attention and validation, like deep down you just want people to tell you you're pretty and cool and worthy, pause. We say this with love: close this book, and go to therapy. Seriously. Social media will *never* fill that void, and it's not a replacement for healthy self-esteem. If you're chasing likes just to feel good about yourself, you'll be disappointed. Turning to social media for emotional validation is like running on a hamster wheel. You keep thinking you'll reach some magical finish line where you "finally feel good," but you'll never reach it. We've seen it happen time and time again.

But if your goal is something tangible, like building a sustainable income, growing an audience around your passion, or creating a platform that opens new opportunities, then this book will help you achieve it.

If now you're thinking, *Ugh, I have no idea what my goal is,* don't freak out. We've got you.

Sometimes you don't know what you want until you see it laid out in front of you.

So here's a list of possible goals to help you brainstorm.

- **Grow your business.** Use social media to promote your existing business or launch a new one.
- **Start a side hustle.** Maybe you want to make an extra $1K a month, then work your way up to $5K, $10K, or even $20K a month.
- **Get free stuff from brands.** Who doesn't love free PR packages?
- **Sell something.** This could be a digital product (like an eBook, app, or digital course), a physical product (like jewelry, candles, or clothing), or a service (like photography, hairstyling, or graphic design).
- **Switch careers.** Maybe you want to use social media to pivot into a new industry, such as writing, acting, modeling, or even becoming a thought leader in your field.
- **Land a creative opportunity.** Maybe you want to pitch a TV show to Netflix, make your own movie, get cast in a film, or have your art in a gallery. Social media can open those doors.
- **Get a record deal.** If you're a musician or singer, growing your following can help you catch the attention of labels.
- **Publish a book.** A built-in audience makes it much easier to land a book deal. You could also self-publish and still sell a bunch of copies.

- **Book speaking engagements.** Want to get paid to speak at events, conferences, or workshops? Social media can help position you as an expert.
- **Launch a nonprofit or charity.** Use your platform to raise awareness (and money) for a cause you care about.
- **Enter politics.** A strong social media presence can help you run for office or advocate for political change.
- **Just make money from being you.** Maybe you don't have a product or service. Maybe you just want to make a living off brand deals, content creation, and sponsorships. That's valid, too.

This list is by no means exhaustive, so don't stress if you don't see the goal you had in mind. You do you!

Whatever your goals are, make sure you get specific. Say them out loud. Make them real! Because if you don't know what you're aiming for, you'll default to chasing growth with no direction. And you'll never arrive anywhere. If your only goal is "be successful" or "get as big as possible," you'll end up burned out and aimless. But if you have a clear target, like "I want to make $5K a month" or "I want to get a book deal," then you can strategize a way to achieve that goal.

Also, don't stress if your goals shift over time. Your goals will change. Ours definitely did. You might start out wanting to be a full-time influencer and later realize you actually want to pivot to starting a business or working behind the scenes. That's normal. Goals evolve as you gain experience. But having some direction from the start will keep you from spiraling into the "just get as big as possible" trap. Having any direction from the start will get you a lot farther than just winging it and hoping to "blow up." Growth without a clear goal is useless. What's the point of having a million followers if you have no idea why you wanted them in the first place?

So don't make the same mistake we did. Set clear, specific goals before you start posting. Want money? Cool. Want career opportunities? Love that. Want to start a business later? Great. Just don't pretend your goal is "I just want be the best version of myself." (Eye roll.) No, you don't. You want something tangible. Own it. Write it down.

What do you actually want social media to do for you?

Defining Success

Success on social media can be surprisingly hard to define. Not long ago, we were at a birthday party and started chatting with a woman about what we do. We mentioned that we run a YouTube channel together, and she casually asked, "Oh, is it successful?" Without thinking much about it, we both said yes. But later, her question got us wondering. What does that even mean? How do you define success in this space?

When you measure in followers and views

There are plenty of ways. Some people try to measure social media success by counting followers or views. But in our opinion, that's actually one of the worst ways to go about it. We often say that having a lot of followers is like being rich in Monopoly money. You might have a big audience, but that doesn't necessarily indicate that you're successful in a meaningful way.

Maybe you have a lot of followers, but they are only paying attention because you were involved in some scandal, and those followers want a front-row seat to the drama. Maybe you're in a niche that doesn't make much money, no matter how many followers you have. Or maybe you haven't figured out how to turn all the attention you're getting into income. You're putting in the work, but the platforms are paying you next to nothing. And if that's the case, can you truly consider it a success?

When you measure in dollars

So how else can you measure success? The most obvious way is to consider how much money you make. Money is simple. It's a number you can count. But what does it take to earn that money? Did the creator have to stir up drama and broadcast their personal life for clicks? Did they put their family on camera and share their children's most vulnerable moments? Did they miss out on weekends, holidays, and quality time because they were glued to a content schedule?

Some of the top earners on the platform OnlyFans make tens of millions of dollars a year. That puts them in the same income bracket as A-list movie stars like Leonardo DiCaprio or Scarlett Johansson. Sounds incredible, right? But then you have to ask yourself what they had to do to make that kind of money. Is that something you'd be willing to do? What lines are you comfortable crossing in the pursuit of income?

And what happens if you try something like OnlyFans, then later decide it's not for you? That's a decision that would be difficult to undo. It might affect your future career, your relationships, and how people see you, sometimes for the rest of your life. Success isn't just about money. There was a time when a lot of other YouTubers started making more risqué content. They posted videos in which they discussed their sex lives or got drunk, just because that kind of content got a lot of views. We didn't want to go down that path, and we think our channel took a hit because of it. Our more wholesome content suddenly looked boring in comparison to our peers.

We also never felt comfortable putting our personal lives on display just to boost engagement. We tried to keep most of our real life off social media. Looking back, this probably hurt our growth and income. It probably made it harder for the audience to feel connected to us in the way they did with more open creators.

Even so, we stand by those choices.

When you measure in hours

There's also the work/life balance to consider. Are you really successful if every weekend and holiday is spent filming content until you're completely burned out?

For years, it became a running joke between us that we always worked on Thanksgiving. No matter how many times we promised ourselves we'd take the day off, something would come up. We'd end up filming or editing while everyone else was relaxing with family. Every year we swore that next year would be different. And every year, it wasn't.

To be clear, we were grateful for the work. And most of the time, we didn't mind. But eventually, you start to ask yourself, where is the line? When do you stop and create boundaries?

This isn't something that only happens in social media. It can happen in any field. Think of the classic stereotype of the business executive dad who is always working and never makes it to his kid's baseball games.

For us, success doesn't mean a consistent grind of hustle and burnout.

Success, your version

Our definition of success includes protecting our privacy and creating content that makes us proud. To be successful is to build a life that feels good to live, one that reflects our values, not just our numbers.

Success looks different for everyone. You have to ask yourself what it really means to you. For some people, success might mean earning a full-time living from social media, even if that income isn't huge. Maybe it's enough to support yourself doing something you love. That alone is a big deal. This book is about how you can turn your social media into real opportunities. And that doesn't always mean making money directly from your audience. You might grow a following and use that to land a hosting job on TV, voice a character in a video game, or get hired for something completely unexpected.

As you read this book, keep this question at the front of your mind: What does success look like to you?

Finding Your Niche

You've decided you want to be a content creator. But what kind of content should you create? What do you actually want to post about?

We've been there! When we first started out, we dabbled in just about everything—beauty, fashion, lifestyle, dating advice, feminine health information, comedy skits, pranks. Our content strategy was basically to just try it all and see what sticks. And, honestly, that's not a bad place to start.

You don't have to have it all figured out on day one. Testing different types of content is part of the process. Every post teaches you something—about your audience, your voice, or even just what you *enjoy* making.

When we taught a social media seminar at the University of Southern California School of Cinematic Arts, the most common questions students asked were things like "How do I figure out what to post?" and "What if I outgrow the type of content I start with?" and "How do I balance quality and consistency?" One of the simplest—but somehow also the hardest—parts of being a creator is figuring out what the hell to post. The first step is figuring out your niche.

Post first, pivot later

Sometimes, having too many choices can actually work against you. It's like going to The Cheesecake Factory. You take one look at that twenty-page menu and suddenly you're overwhelmed and flustered, and you still end up ordering the same thing you always do. (Or is that just us?) Compare that to your experience at a hole-in-the-wall restaurant with a one-page menu. So simple! Lunch is served, no existential crisis on the side.

For better or for worse, your options for content creation are like the menu at The Cheesecake Factory. If you're not careful, you'll overthink yourself into *never* posting anything. You'll spend hours debating between five ideas, burn yourself out tweaking captions and camera angles, and never hit publish. Overthinking kills creativity. You'll become so fixated on the idea of perfection that taking a step in any direction feels like a major permanent deal.

True, there *is* a certain permanence to putting things online. To borrow a line from the film *The Social Network*, "The internet's not written in pencil; it's written in ink." But if you make some content that you're later embarrassed by and want to scrub clean, you can just delete it and move on. At the end of the day, if you want the reward, you have to be willing to risk a little imperfection. Perfection is the enemy of progress. We are *huge* believers in staying flexible. But you need to take that first step and just start posting. You can always pivot later.

Most people hate this advice because they want to get it all "right" from the beginning. That's understandable. We felt the same way. But that's like saying, "I'm moving to England! Which city should I live in for the rest of my life?" when you've never even *been* to England. How would you know if you belong in London or in a cottage in the Cotswolds? You've got to explore a bit. The same goes for content.

People also hate this advice because it means they have to put in more work. If you could do everything perfectly from the beginning, you'd never need to learn, create, invent, or explore. No need to push yourself. But unfortunately, that's just not realistic. To get better at something, you need to practice. To learn how to post better content, you need to spend time creating and posting content, even when it's not perfect.

You might think you love a certain niche, that is, until you actually start making it. You might realize, "Wait . . . this sucks," or "This is way harder than I thought." That's not failure. That's clarity. You won't know what's right for you until you actually try it.

Test before you invest

When we first started out on YouTube over a decade ago, beauty product reviews and makeup tutorials were all the rage. They didn't look that hard to do, and after all, you could reuse the same products over and over again to create new looks. We saw content creators specializing in makeup tutorials, such as Michelle Phan and Tati Westbrook, securing huge opportunities and mainstream recognition. So we decided to jump on the bandwagon.

But first, we needed to upgrade our equipment, and that equipment did not come cheap. We started to think that maybe we should get a new camera lens that could shoot close-up shots in high definition. When you're watching a video of someone applying eyeshadow, you want to see a crisp close-up shot of their eye. Most cameras can't get that kind of shot without a separate lens. Thankfully, before dropping $500 (or more) on a specialty lens, we decided to actually test the waters and shoot a few makeup tutorials first. And thank goodness we did, because that's when we realized we just weren't that into it.

We found makeup tutorials tedious and boring. We don't just mean they were boring to film; they were also boring to edit, and most importantly, ours were boring as hell to watch. We had no innate passion for or interest in makeup tutorials. We decided we didn't want to become the makeup tutorial queens of YouTube, and so we had to find a different path.

Throughout our careers as content creators, we still occasionally did a few makeup tutorials here and there, usually when it was a collaboration with a brand or when we were angling to get one. But we never purchased the specialty lens. We decided our current cameras were good enough for those one-off videos. We actually tried to make up for the lack of expensive lens by making the shots look more dynamic and interesting by shooting using multiple camera angles. We also gave the tutorials more personality by chatting through them, sharing funny stories to hold the viewers' attention and distract them from the fact that we weren't doing ultra close-ups. It worked out fine because it wasn't our niche. Ultimately, we're grateful we didn't waste a lot of money on it. So before you start buying a bunch of supplies or making big changes, take your idea for a test drive. You might not need the new equipment, wardrobe, or props. You might even realize that you want to go in a different direction altogether.

Don't always jump on the bandwagon

When deciding on your niche, it's important to follow your passions but also not to get too swept up in trends. We remember the slime craze from a few years ago. It seemed like overnight, everyone started making homemade slime using Elmer's Glue and contact lens solution. We didn't have a strong interest in making slime, but we had some success in the past with DIY videos. Shanna is pretty crafty and Marissa has a lot of unique ideas, so we would occasionally make DIY videos such as DIY Christmas presents, back-to-school supplies, and Valentine's Day gifts. DIY videos tend to be more complicated for us to film because they require a lot of planning, shopping for supplies, and shooting from different camera angles. So we didn't make them too often.

When slime videos were trending, we didn't have a big urge to jump on board. Maybe because it looked messy, maybe because it felt juvenile, maybe because there was already a ton of excellent content out there that we didn't want to compete with, or maybe simply because we just didn't feel passionately about it. We tried to ignore the trend at first, but it didn't die down—it only got more pervasive. Eventually, we succumbed to the pressure and made a slime video. It ended up being an epic fail.

Unknowingly, we didn't buy the correct ingredients. We thought it wouldn't be a big deal if we cut corners and used a generic brand of glue instead of Elmer's. Something was off with the ingredients so the slime didn't come out correctly. As we edited the footage, we could hear ourselves complaining off camera, "What's going on with the slime? Why isn't the slime working?" In the end, we were so frustrated, burned out, and eager to wrap up filming the video that we just showed some store-bought slime.

In retrospect, we probably should have just owned up to the mistake and instead titled the video some clickbait thing like "Slime gone wrong! Oh no! What happened?" But instead, we just faked it. When we posted the video, there were a few comments here and there calling us out. (They had also tried to make slime using the generic glue and knew it didn't work.) We didn't feel good about the video, it didn't perform well, and the negative comments reinforced what we already knew: slime wasn't for us.

We were relieved to put the slime away and go back to the DIYs that were more fun for us, like chocolate-covered Oreos and homemade cake pops!

Yes, research is great. But sometimes the ideas in your head don't match the reality. And that's okay. You're not carving your niche in stone—you're *finding* it. And finding takes some wandering.

Your content will grow with you

Most creators don't start with a perfectly defined brand. And even if they do, it rarely stays the same. Scroll all the way back on your favorite influencer's page and you'll probably see a completely different person. Different style, different tone, different niche. That's not a glitch in the system. That *is* the system.

Your content will shift over time, and not just because trends change or the algorithm demands sacrifice. You change, too.

Take us, for example. We started out in the lifestyle space, posting a little bit of everything: beauty, outfits, relatable bits. But it wasn't until we leaned into dating advice that we started to see real traction. Then, we ended up making content about menstruation and women's health for a younger audience. We thought we were talking to sixteen to twenty-two-year-olds, but it turned out that the majority of our main audience was much, much younger.

And here's the thing no one warns you about: sometimes your audience finds *you,* not the other way around. That can be great, until you realize you've built a booming content machine for a group you're no longer aligned with. Marissa was graduating college. Shanna was already a few years out. Yet we were deep in the world of tween period problems and middle school girl talk.

Did the content perform well? Yup. Did it make money? Also yup. Did we start to feel a little out of place in our own corner of the internet? Definitely.

Being flexible is one of the biggest lessons, one of the hardest. Especially when you've found something that "works." It takes guts to pivot. It's like walking away from a well-paying job that drains your soul. Not easy.

We asked content creator Amber Scholl, who has built more than 3 million YouTube followers with her DIYs, vision boards, and over-the-top international shopping hauls, how she found her niche on social media. She told us, "My content is genuinely just what I would want to look at—which is a very girly aesthetic. Since I started out, I was always very relatable. People got to see me evolve. I think they look at my content and think 'If she could make it, I can, too.' I'm still the same girl sitting in her bedroom making videos. I just have a much cooler bedroom now."

Amber has some advice for new content creators: "JUST DO IT. Start. Post what you like . . . it's important to love what you post because it takes a ton of time and effort. Numbers should never be the goal, sharing should be. Connection is the heart of it all."

Success needs stamina more than nonstop excitement

If there is such a thing as a "perfect niche," it would be something that you love making and audiences love watching. Simple as that. If you can get close on both of those things, you're ahead of the game. Maybe you don't love making that kind of content 100 percent of the time. But if the content is successful and you like making it 75 percent of the time, that's good enough.

No, you don't need to be obsessed with the kind of content you create (spoiler: you won't be). But if it makes you miserable, that's a red flag.

We once heard about a woman who made a fortune selling online Excel courses. While we respect the hustle, we'd rather chew glass than sell Excel courses, even if it made us rich.

The bottom line is you don't need to be "passionate" about your niche in a capital-P, Pinterest-board way. But you do need to care enough to keep showing up. And you have to care enough to *want* to get better at it.

Because eventually, it's not just about what performs, it's about what lasts.

Estrella Serrato, Mexican American host of the podcast *Cafecito con Estrellita*, which guides first-generation students through higher education, remembers her journey when she first started figuring out what kind of content she wanted to make.

"I started out doing guest blogs, and I noticed that every article I wrote related to higher education in some way. I just made content about things I was interested in, and I finally realized I need to not feel embarrassed! Eventually, I made a podcast episode on the difference between the California State and University of California education systems, and it just blew up! So that inspired me to keep going. I told myself that even if I don't have the best setup, or best equipment or don't have the right look, I can still put myself and my content out there."

Doing Some Soul Searching

If you're totally stuck on what kind of content to make, let's take a step back. Sometimes the best way to figure out what you want to create is to stop thinking like a content strategist and start thinking like your younger self. Take a moment to think about who you were before the noise, before the pressure, before the world told you who to be. Reflect on who you were before the outside world began to shape you. Tap into your inner child. That version of you was creative and curious, and hadn't yet been crushed by algorithm anxiety.

Take yourself for a long walk or listen to some music while pondering over the following questions.

- What did you love doing as a kid? (Did you choreograph dances in your bedroom? Did you make up fake commercials in the mirror? Teach your stuffed animals algebra?)
- What are you naturally good at?

- What do other people always compliment you on or say you're great at?
- What was your favorite subject in school?
- What made you feel excited or lit up?
- What could you talk about for hours without getting bored?
- When you received presents on your birthday or Christmas, what were the most memorable or impactful gifts you ever received?
- What kind of pop culture were you obsessed with growing up? Did you live for Disney Channel dramas, emo music videos, magazine quizzes, Y2K fashion, or early YouTube chaos? All of that stuff is fair game.

A Sampler Platter: Social Media Content Categories Edition

Maybe try to think of your content niche like a buffet. You don't have to stick to just one dish. Wander around, take a look, and see what catches your eye. Maybe something will spark a tiny jolt of curiosity. Just follow what excites you and see where it leads! You're experimenting. Tasting. Gathering data. Some ideas will be a one-and-done bite; others might earn a spot on your plate for good. Just follow what excites you, pay attention to what actually satisfies you, and see where it leads. The best combos are often discovered when you stop overthinking the menu and just start sampling.

We've created a big list of niche social media content categories to get your wheels turning. These ideas run the gamut from personal to professional to entertaining to educational. Even if you already have a clear idea of what you want to make content about, read through these ideas and see what jumps out at you.

Personal and Lifestyle

- Daily routines (morning/night routines, Sunday resets)
- Vlogs or "day in the life" content
- Home decor/room makeovers
- Fashion and OOTDs (outfit of the day)
- Minimalism/maximalism/aesthetic living
- Productivity tips, planners, and to-do lists
- Wellness and mental health check-ins
- Book reviews or reading challenges
- Travel diaries and local recommendations
- Theme parks (like Disney)

Educational and Informational

- "How-to" tutorials or guides
- Myth-busting in your field
- Industry insights (tech, finance, education, and so on)
- Mini history lessons or deep dives
- Explanatory videos (like "What is inflation?" or "How does AI work?")
- Study hacks or language learning tips
- Personal finance/budgeting advice
- Résumé and job search tips
- Academic or career storytelling

Creative and Artistic

- Art process videos/time lapses
- Graphic design or digital illustration

- Photography tips or before-and-after content
- DIYs or crafts (especially aesthetic or visually satisfying ones)
- Poetry, journaling, or creative writing
- Music covers or original songs
- Dance, choreography, or trending challenges
- Behind-the-scenes of a creative process

Entertainment and Humor

- Skits or characters
- Relatable comedy/POV videos
- Reaction content/duets
- Parodies or pop culture commentary
- Memes and trending audio usage
- Hot takes or unpopular opinions
- Pet content with voiceovers

Specialized Communities and Passions

- Astrology, tarot, or spiritual content
- Fandom breakdowns (Taylor Swift theories, Marvel debates, and so on)
- Vintage shopping or thrift store hauls
- Gaming and live-streaming
- Food reviews or restaurant recommendations
- Anime/K-drama commentary
- Conspiracy theories and rabbit holes
- True crime storytelling

Beauty, Fashion, and Wellness

- Get Ready with Me (GRWM) videos
- Skincare routines or product reviews
- Makeup tutorials/transformations
- Fashion hauls or styling tips
- Haircare and salon content
- Fitness routines or postpartum workouts
- Meal prepping or "what I eat in a day"
- Hormonal health or menstruation advice

Thoughtful and Reflective

- Life advice/things you've learned
- Journal prompts
- Storytimes (embarrassing, inspiring, or ridiculous)
- Lessons from therapy or self-help books
- Faith/spirituality and mindfulness practices
- Parenting reflections or adulting confessions

Business and Branding

- Behind-the-scenes of running a business
- Building a personal brand
- Small business packaging/order fulfillment
- Customer testimonials or reviews
- Growth milestones and transparent income reports
- Tips for creators, freelancers, or founders
- Pitching to brands or negotiating deals

These are just a handful of the countless niches that exist online. Seriously, if you can think it, there's probably already a community for it. Whether you're into travel, fashion, food, gaming, or something super specific (like competitive cheerleading or sourdough bread baking), we hope this list sparks some inspiration. Use it as a jumping-off point to start brainstorming your own corner of the internet.

And remember, you don't need to commit to just one niche. Pick a few that genuinely interest you, even if they seem totally unrelated. Jot them down, then do a little digital digging. Check out creators who are posting in those spaces. If it's something you're into, chances are you're already following a few without even realizing it.

Scroll through their content and take some mental notes. What do you love? What would you do differently? Let your impressions inspire you and start writing down your own video ideas. Once you've got a big list, highlight the ones that feel the most doable and exciting. That's your launchpad.

Remember, finding your niche isn't about locking yourself into one perfect idea. It's about giving yourself permission to explore, try things, and test out topics. Keep what works, drop what doesn't, and pay attention to what feels sustainable, not just successful. Your niche isn't a box you step into; it's a path you carve by showing up, experimenting, and evolving. So load up your plate, trust your instincts, and remember, you'll figure it out one post at a time.

2

Going Viral

We started making YouTube videos in 2012. Although we spent years consistently putting out videos, we grew painfully slowly, not seeing much success. After three years of work, the countless hours we'd invested grew us to a modest follower count of around 30,000, a commendable yet hardly groundbreaking figure. Though faced with moments of discouragement, the idea of quitting never entered our minds.

In late 2015, we made a pivotal decision to overhaul our content strategy entirely, and the results were nothing short of phenomenal. Within a few weeks, our channel experienced a huge burst of growth. This transformation required a carefully calculated departure from the status quo. Previously, we had had a few "one-hit wonder" videos here and there, but our channel as a whole wasn't especially popular. After we paused and carefully studied what was winning and what wasn't, we were able to grow our channel significantly without losing momentum.

This knowledge became the driving force behind our continued success. The ability to replicate our achievements became second nature, leading us to milestones like 50K followers, a subsequent doubling to 100K two months later, and an increase to 200K shortly thereafter. About a year later, our follower count soared to one million.

Throughout our journey, we've had the privilege of speaking at esteemed venues like Google HQ, YouTube Space, University of Southern California (USC), and TEDx, and sharing our insights with aspiring content creators. The burning question on everyone's mind when we tell our story is always the same: How did we achieve our explosive growth? What were the pivotal changes we made after years of a slow climb to a modest follower count? Our audiences consistently yearned for the elusive "ultimate secret" for going viral. People were eager for that one magic tip, the easy-to-follow recipe, or the secret sauce that would catapult them into the social media stratosphere.

We remember once during a creator panel at YouTube Space, where we spoke alongside prominent creators like Sazan Hendrix, Jorge Narvaez of Reality Changers, and Meghan Tonjes. The audience was a more intimate gathering of about fifty aspiring content creators, and we felt comfortable with the crowd. When asked about our remarkable channel growth, Shanna jokingly responded, "It's so easy. The big secret is just posting your content at 2 PM every day."

Immediately, the energy in the room shifted, and some faces became serious, as if they believed we were unveiling the clandestine YouTube algorithm for going viral. A man in his forties running an educational channel who was sitting in the front row suddenly leaned forward with intensity, demanding to know if that really was the secret. We laughed a bit, nervously, and hastily backtracked, assuring the crowd we were just kidding.

Despite our attempt to inject humor, the exchange highlighted the persistent desire for a straightforward answer. Unfortunately, in content creation, there's no equivalent to a quick fix, and even supposed shortcuts come with their own complexities and drawbacks.

The reality of our journey was that there wasn't a singular, easy secret. There were dozens of things we started doing differently, simultaneously, that propelled our amazing growth. We wish we could tell you it was as simple as directing people to "post at 2 PM" but unfortunately, our strategy was far more intricate than that. In social media's ever-changing landscape, stagnation equates to irrelevance. Going viral requires staying attuned to emerging trends, anticipating shifts, and being agile in adjusting your content strategy. The secret isn't just in the content itself; it's also in the adaptability and foresight to ride the waves of social media evolution.

In this chapter, we delve into the specific adjustments we made, uncovering the multifaceted nature of our success. We'll explore how these lessons can be applied to your own journey, recognizing that success in the dynamic world of social media requires a nuanced and comprehensive approach.

Do What You're Good At

Identifying our unique strengths was a key part of our strategic overhaul. Comedy and advice for young females emerged as our forte. We recognized that not everyone can master comedy or deliver advice effectively, so we leveraged these strengths to our advantage.

We experimented regularly with new topics, from pranks and paranormal content to DIY and beauty, which allowed us to tap into our multifaceted capabilities.

But how do you know what you're good at? Discovering your strengths and defining your niche is a journey of exploration (one that we guide you through in chapter 1). No one has all the answers right from the start. It's a process of trial and error, so experiment with ideas and categories until a clear winner or a few standout areas emerge. By actively trying out different content styles, you figure out what resonates with you as a creator. Pay attention to the content that feels fulfilling to produce, bringing out your passion and creativity. Simultaneously, observe how your audience responds, gauging the engagement, comments, and overall reception. It's through this dynamic process of experimentation that your niche begins to crystallize.

It also helps to keep a running list of potential content ideas. When we decided to overhaul our channel, we started keeping notebooks full of extensive lists of video ideas. Some of the videos required a cast of fifty extras, drone footage, complex editing that would take weeks to figure out, and thousands of dollars in supplies. So not every idea came to fruition because, realistically, we didn't have the time, resources, or budget. But that's not the point. Those notebooks ensured that we never faced a shortage of inspiration.

It's Not All About You

While your personal preferences matter, the crux of success lies in delivering what your audience craves and aligning with the algorithms of the platforms you engage with. Don't just create the content you want to make. You need to make content that other people want to see.

One fundamental change we made was shifting from creating self-indulgent videos that solely interested us to crafting content that resonated with our audience's desires. At the time, a popular trend among creators was getting "tagged" to answer lists of personal questions. The questions ranged from things like your favorite color, your birthday, or what you were wearing. Those sorts of videos were fun to make but not compelling to *watch*. Instead of posting whatever we felt like sharing in the moment, we began asking ourselves better questions: Were we providing value? Were we entertaining? Were we giving people something worth their time? Every piece of content became a thoughtful consideration of our audience's needs. Deliberately shaping our content to resonate with our audience allowed us to foster a community that not only consumed but actively engaged with our content.

Home in on who you want your audience to be and make every decision with them in mind. Be specific with those demographics. Do you want to appeal to college-aged young women? Men who love tech? Foodies? Then give those people what they want! Start by studying the content they already gravitate toward. Don't limit your research to social media, but look everywhere they're consuming: digital magazines, news outlets, newsletters, popular TV shows, and podcasts. Pay attention to the patterns. What do these pieces of content have in common? Is it the tone? The structure? The topics? The humor? Once you spot those threads, weave them into your own content in a way that feels authentic to you.

Keep Your Finger on the Pulse

To stay ahead of the game, we immersed ourselves in the content landscape, regularly consuming content and actively observing what resonated. We did plenty of research using tools like Google Trends to gauge the pulse of popular interests.

We focused in on trending topics and seasonal topics. The winter holidays and back-to-school emerged as our prime "seasons." We strategically prepared for these peaks, crafting videos weeks or even months in advance to position ourselves ahead of the curve. Our meticulously planned content calendar allowed us not only to follow trends but to set them, ensuring our content remained timely and resonated with our audience's ever-changing interests.

Learn from the Competition

A soccer coach once told me, "If you want to win the game, start by studying the players already scoring goals." When we decided to reinvent our channel, we started with a simple question: Who was already doing something similar, but actually doing it well? We curated a list of about fifty creators who were similar to us—primarily young women in their twenties producing lifestyle content.

Our fastest growing platform was YouTube, so we devised a competitive analytics strategy for other YouTube creators. We'd go through each creator on the list, pull up their YouTube channel, and look at two metrics.

Firstly, we delved into their top-performing videos of all time, spanning years, to identify evergreen ideas. Secondly, we scrutinized their recent successes, examining the past month, the past three months, or the past six months, depending on their posting frequency. Generally, we'd analyze their last thirty videos or so. While occasionally watching videos, we primarily focused on titles, thumbnails, and view counts, aiming to discern stylistic elements that contributed to their success. Our objective was not to replicate but to identify strategies that led to success.

Learning from our competitors proved invaluable in developing our own distinctive style. We understood the importance of borrowing insights from others while infusing our unique touch into the content landscape.

You can do this, too. Start by making a short list of creators in your niche. Chances are, many of them are already in your feed. Look at who they follow, who they collaborate with, and who they're frequently tagged alongside. Explore relevant hashtags, and pay attention to the recommended creators that appear after you follow someone. You can even find inspiration by looking at the creators followed by certain PR agencies in your space.

Once you have your list, start doing your own competitive analysis. Keep track of video ideas that stand out to you, and take note of the patterns that emerge. What topics keep coming up? What formats are being repeated? What hooks or angles seem to perform well? Over time, you'll start uncovering real insight.

Your Quality Can Always Be Better

Elevating the caliber of our videos was a transformative step. We adopted the perspective of an audience member, ensuring our content was short, attention-grabbing, and value-driven. We focused not only on delivering valuable information but also on creating entertainment.

In our early days, we embraced a DIY ethos, creating makeshift sets and sourcing colorful pillows from the dollar store for background décor in our videos. For lighting, we balanced desk lamps on stacks of cardboard boxes. Not everyone can afford top-tier equipment when they first start out, and our journey reflects that reality. When we made it to about 200,000 subscribers, we started earning more money, so we decided that it was time to invest in better equipment and supplies. We upgraded our camera equipment and finally purchased some proper lighting. It was a game changer!

While you may not start with state-of-the-art equipment, there comes a point at which upgrading your resources improves your content so much that it becomes worth the cost.

Focus on the Intro

Our research taught us that the first few seconds of any video are crucial. Incentivizing viewers to stay until the end is awesome, but nothing surpasses the impact of those first moments. To make the most of our video intros, we started making them shorter, snappier, and infused with high energy. We also strategically placed our best tips and most captivating content right at the beginning.

Get Passive Viewers to Take Action

Many creators include *calls to action* in their content. This is when you tell the viewer to do something, whether it's clicking a link, following you, giving the video a thumbs up, or leaving a comment. If your content is a photo instead of a video, calls to action will be in the form of text, either written across the photo (as in Instagram stories) or written in the caption.

Clear calls to action became a cornerstone of our videos, strategically placed at the beginning and end to guide our audience's engagement.

When we decided to overhaul our channel, converting viewers into subscribers became a strategic goal for us. With each click on our video, we aimed to build a community of active supporters. We would always provide a call to action at the beginning and end of the video, but we quickly realized that this wasn't enough. We recognized that the generic "like and subscribe" plea had become a ubiquitous feature in every influencer's video. Audiences had grown to tune it out like white noise.

To break through the monotony, we came up with creative and engaging ways to get viewers' attention, amuse them, and encourage action. Instead of relying on the conventional plea, we found success in presenting specific numerical goals, like "Let's aim for 10,000 thumbs ups on this video!" or "My goal is to reach 10,000 followers!" By sharing our aspirations, we discovered that the audience was more inclined to actively help us achieve these milestones. People crave connection and enjoy contributing to other people's success. Also, if you tell your audience that you are aiming for a specific number of likes/comments, it gives the audience something to strive for. They'll also be able to see how they're helping you reach that goal.

In addition to setting numerical goals, we moved beyond the mundane and introduced quirky, humorous incentives to encourage subscriptions. These incentives were tailored to the video's tone, injecting an element of fun into the engagement process. For instance, in a "Holiday Gift Guide" video, we playfully promised that "The first 1,000 people to like this video will find money on the floor today!" In a video about "Period Life Hacks," we said, "Like this video if you want to have a light, easy period! Don't you want to have an easy period with no cramps? I know I sure do!" Having these quirky little "chain mail" type of positive things attached to liking the video gets the audience involved and gives something to talk about. Also, superstition and curiosity are great motivators, causing them to like the video, because most people like to believe in good luck.

While it may sound gimmicky, our audience, primarily young women, embraced the playful nature of these incentives. It transformed the routine request into an interesting and interactive experience, as evident in the comments section, where viewers shared whether the lighthearted predictions had come true. This approach may not suit every content creator, but for us, it created a dynamic and participatory connection with our audience.

Determine the Best Time to Post

Our obsession with analytics led us to leverage platform-provided data, allowing us to pinpoint the optimal date and time for posting. Capitalizing on the trend of active weekend viewership, we strategically unveiled our best, most viral-worthy content on Fridays, Saturdays, and Sundays, sort of like a TV network putting its hit show with the highest ratings in the primetime spot. Mid-week became our experimental playground, reserved for riskier or more casual videos with lower production values.

Ask yourself: Where does your audience live, and what time zone are they in? When do your people go online? Does your audience work a nine-to-five? Do they go to school during the day? Put careful thought into when to launch your content and use your analytics to figure out when your target audience is online. Test out different days and times until you find what works for you.

Make It Easy to Be Found

We became very good at tagging videos and stuffing our descriptions with keywords, turning each video into a highly discoverable little gem. We became much more strategic with our titles, focusing on keyword-rich and attention-grabbing phrases. Should our video titles be in all capital letters? All lowercase? Should the titles be long? Short? We were constantly experimenting, tweaking, and adjusting depending on what was and wasn't working.

As YouTube's policies evolved, we learned not to get too attached to one set way of doing things. For instance, we witnessed a shift in which all-caps titles, once considered effective, were labeled as clickbait. Staying aware of such changes and understanding how platform policies influence content visibility became integral to our strategy.

Try Out Different Video Lengths

On social media, every second counts, and learning to keep viewers hooked became a game changer. Content length is a perpetually shifting metric, demanding constant adaptation. When we first started out, most YouTube videos ran about five to seven minutes long. However, the landscape transformed as YouTube sought to rival television, prompting an era in which longer videos, spanning fifteen to twenty minutes, were encouraged to boost watch time, a vital demographic.

The digital realm, however, is anything but static. In 2020, short-form content surged, with videos under a minute long gaining precedence. By late 2025, TikTok was prioritizing videos over one minute long.

How fast or slow you speak can also impact the audience's attention spans. Taking cues from YouTube insights, we learned that creators who spoke faster enjoyed higher watch times. A person normally uses 100 to 150 words per minute in casual conversation, but on YouTube, the sweet spot is 170 to 180 words per minute. Acknowledging our different speaking paces, we adjusted our delivery to maintain a brisk pace, ensuring the audience remained captivated and less likely to click away. Any pauses we took while speaking were cut out in the editing room.

Explore the Unexplored

Another effective strategy for going viral is to home in on subjects that other creators have overlooked and are not yet oversaturated. In our case, we delved into women's health content, recognizing its high online search demand coupled with a scarcity of video creators addressing the topic. It's a common misconception that every conceivable topic has been covered online; in reality, numerous untapped subjects await discovery.

Sometimes a topic has been covered, but not well. Sometimes great content exists but is hard to find. Sometimes it's discoverable but isn't informative or entertaining. Confused? The takeaway is simple: there's always room for your unique perspective. By finding the gaps and bringing your voice to subjects others have overlooked, you can create content that stands out and resonates with viewers.

We also started creating prank videos, a topic dominated mainly by men. Prank videos were already proven crowd-pleasers, but the unique twist of having a woman take the lead added a fresh and entertaining dynamic. That enabled us to carve a distinctive niche for ourselves in a space where such content was not yet prevalent.

The key takeaway here is the power of identifying subjects that haven't been exhaustively explored. Don't assume that every idea has been taken. There are still uncharted territories waiting to be explored. Even if you do feel like a subject has been covered already, it hasn't been covered by you; perhaps you will deliver it in a new, fresh, and exciting way that the internet hasn't seen before. It's through tapping into these niches that you can not only offer something novel to your audience but also position yourself as a trailblazer in the ever-evolving landscape of social media content.

Merge Education with Entertainment

Crafting compelling content hinges on understanding your audience and delivering value. When creating, ask yourself: Are you entertaining people? Are you teaching them something? The real magic happens when you seamlessly blend education and entertainment.

Our rise in popularity was marked by the realization that the market lacked engaging content on certain topics, particularly menstruation advice for young women. The only other period videos that existed online at the time were either overly didactic and dull or comedic in a way that often ridiculed or shamed women. Recognizing this gap, we pioneered a strategy that combined education and entertainment.

The fusion of these two elements became our secret sauce for going viral. And this method isn't limited to specific niches! It's a universal approach applicable to diverse content genres, including yours.

Regardless of the type of content you create, the key lies in delivering valuable information in an entertaining package. Whether you're imparting knowledge about the latest gadgets or showcasing delectable recipes, combining entertainment with education emerges as a fail-safe strategy. It not only captures your audience's attention but also positions you as a source of both information and enjoyment.

Feed the Beast!

You can't go viral if you don't post consistently, full stop.

You may roll your eyes at this advice, but "Be consistent" is a mantra that, despite its predictability, stands as the cornerstone of success. The rhythm of consistent posting not only keeps your audience engaged but also aligns with algorithms' hunger for fresh, regular content.

In the dynamic world of social media, where trends shift like the wind, consistency is your ally. But it's not just about mindlessly churning out content. To make the algorithm work for you, you need to understand your analytics. That demands agility, an ability to adapt to the nuances of what the algorithms crave. Whether it's capitalizing on trending audio or diving into conversations around popular subjects, staying attuned to the pulse of the online world is crucial.

Check which of your posts get the most views, watch time, likes, comments, and shares. Assess metrics like watch time, engagement rate, click-through rate, and audience retention. Look for patterns. Are shorter videos keeping people watching longer? Do certain topics spark more engagement? Use this information to make decisions. Repeat what works and adjust what doesn't.

Identify high-growth periods when the algorithm is favoring your content, and seize the momentum. Embrace the busy periods, and, if necessary, consider outsourcing tasks like editing to maintain the flow. While the prospect of hiring help might seem daunting, it can be a strategic move to enhance productivity and unlock growth beyond the limits of individual capabilities.

Set Goals You Can Keep

How much do I post? How often do I post? Which platforms do I post on? The dilemma of how frequently to post on social media is a common conundrum for aspiring influencers. Every single platform is vying for your content, and they all encourage you to post daily.

Beware of the relentless push for continuous output from social media platforms. The "post at all costs" mentality can be detrimental to your well-being and creativity, and may lead you down a path of sacrificing personal time and relationships. It's easy to overcommit yourself and end up burning out quickly, especially if you're juggling other commitments like a job, studies, family, or maintaining a social life. It's so important to set boundaries that align with your content creation goals, and it can be the tactic that makes you a successful content creator instead of one that burns out quickly. (See chapter 7 for more on setting boundaries.) Aspiring influencers must be analytical in the initial stages, realistically assessing how much time different kinds of content demand. How long does it take you to create one video from start to finish (including conceptualizing, scripting, filming, editing, and uploading)? How long does it take you to execute a photoshoot or write out a caption?

Be mindful of what fits within your schedule and the time you're willing to invest. Some people start strong for a month and then stop, simply because they bite off more than they can chew. You need to consider your other obligations and determine how much time you can realistically dedicate to your content. Some people will allot ten hours per week to creating and posting content. Some people will allot five minutes, post a hasty shot of their dinner, and then wonder why it didn't go viral.

Opt for a more strategic approach to maximize your time, such as content batching. This involves creating multiple pieces of content in a short period of time that can be spread out over several weeks. Try a mix of high- and low-effort content. We would incorporate sit-and-talk sessions (low effort) with on-the-go skits (high effort), ensuring diversity in our content offerings. Consider outsourcing tasks and tactically delegating time.

Acknowledge the temptation to prioritize quantity over quality and find a balance that aligns with your goals, ensuring that the pursuit of popularity doesn't come at the expense of your well-being. Remember, it's about crafting a sustainable path, not a frenetic race to the next upload.

The "Secret"

So, here we are. Going viral, as it turns out, is a tad more complex than posting at 2 PM. It's no wonder creators get overwhelmed!

Anyone can go viral once through sheer luck, but repeatedly achieving it demands strategic planning and relentless effort. The so-called "secret" isn't a mystical elixir or a magic potion. Going viral is a nuanced dance. It's the amalgamation of numerous well-executed strategies, implemented consistently. It's not about excelling in just one aspect but mastering a multitude of elements consistently and diligently. Always keep the big picture in mind, recognizing that shortcuts may have long-term consequences.

Our journey to social media stardom unfolded through understanding our audience, intentionally leveraging our strengths, and adapting to the ever-shifting content landscape. The secret lies not in a singular action but in considering audience behavior, platform intricacies, and strategic posting. Success on social media is a blend of self-discovery and connection with your audience. Keep experimenting, stay open to evolution, and let the feedback from your audience guide you toward content that not only showcases your talents but also resonates deeply with those who follow your journey.

3

Why You Should Be a Copycat

"Copycat."

It's a word that has such an ugly reputation, doesn't it? When we hear it, we think of someone who lacks originality, someone who can't think for themselves, someone who doesn't have any good ideas.

But what if being a copycat isn't a bad thing, but a powerful strategy? This chapter will challenge you to rethink your preconceived notions about copying.

True originality is rare. The world is saturated with ideas, trends, and content. Almost everything you see online is a remix of something else. But what sets you apart isn't creating something completely new; it's how you make existing ideas your own.

Copying other creators on social media is not only unavoidable, it's a savvy move. The pursuit of pure originality, often glamorized, is, in fact, overrated. It's sometimes wiser to stick with something tried-and-true, drawing from content that has a proven track record of resonating with audiences rather than trying to go rogue and reinvent the wheel.

People want to follow influencers who personally resonate with them. Your voice, your look, and your personality are the unique ingredients that transform something familiar into something fresh and exciting.

Take beauty tutorials, for example. There are countless makeup routines online but viewers typically want to watch beauty influencers who look like themselves. People often assume the beauty space is oversaturated, but that's far from the truth. Viewers gravitate toward influencers who reflect their own physical features. Someone with brown eyes often wants to watch a beauty tutorial meant for brown eyes. Someone with curly hair wants to watch someone else with curly hair. Viewers want to watch someone who represents their beauty standards.

It's not about competing with the most-followed influencers. It's about connecting authentically with your audience. People love beauty videos not just for the techniques, but because they're watching someone who feels relatable, inspiring, or aspirational.

When Pablo Picasso said, "Good artists copy; great artists steal," he meant that great creators don't just mimic. They take inspiration from others, internalize it, and make it their own. A *good* artist might copy another's work exactly as it is, but a *great* artist adds their own spin, transforming the original into something uniquely theirs. The same principle applies to social media. Study the techniques, trends, and styles of top influencers, then adapt them to fit your voice and brand. This isn't about imitation; it's about evolution. Learn from other creators' successes. Learn from their failures. Let them do some market research for you.

How to Steal

How exactly does one steal an idea without copying it? Well, the first step is to consume content with purpose. Inspiration can come from anywhere, whether it's a popular song, a trendy editing trick, or even a color. Watch, listen, and read widely. Notice what grabs your attention and figure out why it works. Then take that spark and make it your own.

Save, save, save!

Save posts, videos, and ideas that resonate with you even if it's about a topic outside of your wheelhouse.

We recommend using folders, notes, a notebook, and screenshots to save (and organize!) the content that inspires you. We frequently screenshot things that catch our eye, and go through the screenshots every few days to revisit inspiring things and curate our ideas. This is something we particularly like to do with trending texts that follow a theme. For example, since Shanna has a baby, we are currently focusing on creating content for new moms. We've collected screenshots of videos that fall into the category of "inspirational new mom" posts. Maybe you're looking for inspiration from funny cat videos, or relatable and imperfect cooking videos. Whatever niche you're in, focus on getting inspo from related videos.

These notes, saves, and screenshots will become your "inspiration bank," which you can refer to when you're planning new projects! Perhaps you've allocated yourself just two hours per week in which to film and edit your videos. But when the time comes to get to work, your mind is blank. You sit there letting the minutes tick by until your time has run out and you haven't accomplished anything. Now you're going to miss your uploading schedule for the week and fall behind. It can be hard to come up with clever ideas on command. This is where your notebook of ideas comes in clutch. Visit your inspiration bank and let your imagination soar.

Learn from similar creators

Follow creators who are either already similar to you, or who you aspire to be like. Study their big-picture business model and analyze which elements you admire. This extends beyond just the content they make. It also applies to potential sponsorships, collaborations, and audience-building strategies. For example, there are probably at least a handful of successful creators out there with whom you have a lot in common. Perhaps you live in the same city, are around the same age, are the same gender, have a similar audience demographic, and make content within the same category. Pay attention to what they do, who they associate with, and what brands they work with. Learn from your competition; they can be your best teachers.

There's a right way to "copy" and a wrong way. The wrong way is trying to be a clone of someone else. The right way is the Picasso way! Learn from others without losing your originality. If another creator has a signature element closely associated with them, like a distinctive hairstyle or recognizable color, avoid copying it. Instead, focus on developing your own signature elements. Maybe it's a cute pet that appears in your videos, a car you like to film in, or a quirky catchphrase you like to say at the beginning or end of your content.

Always put your own spin on things. Take the ideas that resonate, experiment with your own twist, combine multiple influences, and adapt them to your voice and style.

Learn from different creators

Don't make the mistake of ignoring great creators just because they have a different niche or style. We firmly believe that your muse could be a creator who posts content that is completely different from what you post or are interested in. Inspiration can come from anywhere. Whether your focus is automotive, food, fashion, finance, music, gaming, or any other niche, the key lies in borrowing successful elements from unrelated domains. Don't just imitate—innovate.

Borrowing from a different niche can be a game changer. For example, a food influencer could borrow the way a fitness creator films their videos and use it to make recipes more dynamic. A finance creator might use humor like a comedy channel to make budgeting tips easier to digest. The point is, inspiration can come from anywhere. Look outside your own niche and you'll start spotting ideas that others might miss.

Embrace the trend cycle

Social media trends come and go quickly. These trends are what make being a copycat so advantageous. Trends often surge for a day or two. During this time, people are actively searching for the trend, and the algorithms are amplifying it, giving you a prime opportunity to take advantage by jumping on the bandwagon.

Paying attention to what others are doing, whether it's copying trending audio, text, styles, or formats, can give you a significant edge. It also increases your chances of going viral, especially if you can be early enough to a trend, or do it in a bigger, better way than everyone else.

Handling Copycat Drama

It's natural for creators to feel hesitant about closely mirroring someone else's work, fearing potential backlash. Getting publicly called out, while unlikely, is a possibility, and it is not fun.

There was a time when another young lifestyle influencer accused us on Twitter of copying her "DIY Edible Back-to-School Supplies" video. On the surface, we could see how it might have looked that way. Our videos had similar titles and thumbnails, and ours was released a week after hers. But the truth was, we had never seen her channel before, and she wasn't on our radar at all. The video she accused us of copying had been planned for weeks, filmed a month earlier, and involved detailed preparation.

You know how people talk about having "receipts"? We had literal receipts from the store where we had purchased the art supplies for our video—glitter, poster board, candy, and more. We were so tempted to post them and prove our timeline, but we resisted the urge.

Furthermore, we did a little online digging and discovered that she wasn't even the first creator to make that kind of video. DIY Queen Karina Garcia had posted a similar project around five months earlier, showing herself making edible crayons. Funnily enough, we had both unintentionally followed a trend that someone else had started. Even if we had copied her, it really didn't matter. We wanted so badly to put her on blast for publicly attacking us, especially since her video had millions of views while ours had a comparatively modest 100K. But we resisted the urge to fire back. We ignored it. We didn't publicly respond and focused on creating more content instead. Within a couple of days, the drama fizzled out. The ironic part? By the following year, everyone in the DIY space was making "DIY Edible Back-to-School Supplies" videos. What once seemed original ended up becoming a trend that many took part in.

Looking back, we're so glad we didn't react in a way we might regret now. When we google our names, what pops up is a list of our accomplishments, not cringy Twitter drama or some embarrassing beef with another creator. That professionalism speaks louder than any public feud ever could.

We've always been proponents of avoiding embarrassing drama. It's not always the easy thing to do, but we think in the long run, treating yourself like a business pays off. Would a professional business respond to petty drama? Of course not.

If you ever find yourself accused of copying, avoid engaging in heated exchanges. By handling these situations with grace, you show that you value integrity, creativity, and professionalism. Traits that will help you thrive in the long run.

Admittedly, it might have made for entertaining content if we'd "put her on blast" and shown the receipts. Drama sells. Audiences love it and can't get enough of it. But you know who doesn't love drama? Brands. And our income was largely reliant on brand deals. Brands look for creators who align with their values. Brands typically want to put their marketing dollars behind "safe" investments, meaning creators who are drama-free and focused on their craft, not controversies.

If you are running a drama channel, by all means, capitalize on whatever beef comes your way. But that wasn't our lane. Staying focused on creating quality content and maintaining professionalism is what's helped us thrive.

Give Credit Where Credit Is Due

We believe that giving credit isn't always necessary, but if it feels right to you, go for it! If you're inspired by another creator and want to acknowledge them, you can do so by either mentioning them verbally if you're filming a video or adding a note in the description of your photo or written post.

That acknowledgment can be as simple as writing or saying, "Thank you to so-and-so for inspiring this idea!" If you want to take it a step further, you could add a line like "Check out their page for more amazing content!"

Not only is this a great way to show respect, but it can also help you build connections. It can be tricky to make friends online, so one way to get another creator's attention is to tag them in your content. Hopefully, the creator feels flattered instead of competitive. If the creator you credit shares the same audience, their followers may engage with your content as well.

Years ago, we took inspiration from another creator and it backfired. She had made a series of charming YouTube videos imagining Disney princesses interacting in real life. Being lifelong Disney fans ourselves, we loved the whimsical nature of the theme and decided to create our own take on it. We recreated the concept with different princesses and different storylines.

But when the first video finally went live, we received thousands of comments stating some variation of "Rachel did it first! You're copying Rachel!" It became overwhelming at one point, and we had to stop reading the comments.

In hindsight, we wish we had acknowledged that she came up with the idea first. It didn't feel good to have all that effort reduced to a wave of negative comments. It dismissed the hours of work, time, and money we had put into creating our own scripts, buying costumes, and hiring actors. We had even rented professional equipment and a castle to film it all in! Although the majority of comments were positive, the influx of negative comments still stung. We wonder in retrospect if the audience might have appreciated our project as its own thing if we had explicitly acknowledged Rachel's influence. Guess we'll never know!

At the end of the day, creating great content should always be your priority, no matter the feedback you receive. But if you're directly inspired by someone, don't be afraid to acknowledge it. Giving credit shows authenticity and builds trust with your audience.

What About When Others Copy Your Work?

Having someone else copy your work is an interesting feeling. On the one hand, you're proud and flattered to know that you were the trendsetter who inspired others. But on the other hand, you're frustrated when people don't give you credit and act like they invented the idea.

Unfortunately, the frustration and anger can often outweigh the pride, particularly if the person copying you gets more views or recognition than you, the original creator. It's hard not to feel disheartened or angry, but it's important not to let those emotions cloud your judgment.

We find it helpful to view it as a compliment. After all, they say that imitation is the sincerest form of flattery. If people are copying you, it means you are successful and influential. Your creativity is resonating with others.

A few years ago, Marissa invented a fun and original video idea: the Candy Kissing Challenge. Challenges were trending at the time, especially ones you could shoot with your boyfriend or girlfriend. Marissa invented one where one person ate a piece of candy, then kissed their blindfolded significant other. The other person had to guess what kind of candy they ate. The concept was lighthearted, playful, and a hit with our audience. Within days, the video raced to a million views.

Before long, other influencers started jumping on the trend as well, posting their own versions of the Candy Kissing Challenge. At first, we felt frustrated. After all, it was our idea! But over time, we noticed an unexpected benefit. Other creators copying the challenge actually boosted our video's visibility, making it more searchable and increasing our views even further. When multiple creators jump on a trend, it boosts visibility for everyone.

Ultimately, the best thing you can do is rise above the drama. If people are copying what you do, it means that you're setting trends and influencing others. That's a powerful position to be in! Instead of focusing on the frustration, lean into the pride of knowing you're an innovator.

Avoiding Copyright Violations

If someone infringes on a protected piece of intellectual property without permission, that's a different story. For example, if you repost someone else's work without consent or steal someone else's viral video and upload it to your own page, the copyright holder is entitled to file a copyright claim with the platform hosting the stolen content.

From our experience, social media platforms take legal complaints seriously and are usually quick to remove infringing content. Too many infractions will lead to your social media account getting permanently disabled. You don't want to find yourself in the position of having to hire a lawyer and correspond with a platform's legal department asking them to reinstate your account after it's been disabled for too many copyright violations. Protect your own work and respect the intellectual property of others.

Be a Copycat, But Also Be You

The truth is, even if you're inspired by someone else's work, the missing piece is *you*. You are the X Factor. Your face, voice, perspective, background, delivery, and editing style all combine to create something uniquely yours. That's why audiences are drawn to you. Focus on borrowing ideas in a way that inspires your own unique creation. Let other people's work motivate you to innovate rather than imitate. Keep refining and innovating to develop your own signature style.

Being a copycat on social media can be a great thing as long as you don't discount what you uniquely have to offer. Don't fall into the trap of thinking someone else out there is inherently better than you. Recognize and appreciate what you bring to the table and always aim to put your own personal spin on whatever you create.

Zoe Unlimited, a lifestyle and marketing creator, says, "If you copy someone else, you will always be second best. Take what you like but also make it into something new."

Being a copycat isn't about lacking creativity. It's about leveraging the wisdom and success of others to grow and thrive. The internet is a vast playground of ideas waiting for you to make your mark. So, stop worrying about being 100 percent original. Instead, focus on being 100 percent *you* as you take inspiration from the best.

4

Equipment You'll Need

Picture this: we're filming a video in Shanna's bedroom, which is about the size of a large walk-in closet. The only place to sit is the twin bed (the room isn't large enough for a queen). The camera, which was the cheapest refurbished DSLR model sold on Canon's website, is precariously placed on a stack of shoeboxes atop a wobbly TV tray. (We haven't bought a tripod.)

There are a couple of bright desk lamps also perched on strategically positioned cardboard boxes. The bright light bulbs made too much of a harsh, round spotlight, so to soften and diffuse the light a little bit, we tape white tissue paper to the front of the lamp, just an inch or two away from the hot, glowing bulb.

The entire makeshift studio setup in Shanna's tiny bedroom is composed of simple items we found around our house. It looks incredibly haphazard, almost a joke, and our parents groan and roll their eyes each time they see us dragging lamps and boxes into the room. Yet the effect on camera works surprisingly well. It's bright and airy, warm with soft colors. "All that matters is what you end up with on camera," we tell each other.

On this particular day, we're having a longer film shoot, and we've already been at it for a couple of hours. The confined space has grown hot and sweaty. Suddenly, we smell something faintly burning. We glance at our lamps and gasp with alarm. The tissue paper on one of the lamps is browning right in front of the light bulbs—it's moments away from catching on fire!

Marissa leaps up and rips the tissue paper off the lamps, while Shanna runs to unplug the lamps from the wall. The crisis has been averted, but our hearts are still thumping with leftover adrenaline and fear. That was a close one.

The threat of a house fire was enough to scare us into buying some proper filming lamps. We used that makeshift DIY setup for over a year. Every single time we filmed, it was the same process. Stack the boxes perfectly so they don't come crashing down. Tape the tissue paper so that the delicate paper isn't directly touching the hot light bulb. Adjust the position of the lamps to create the perfect lighting effects. And then when we're done filming for the day, tear it all down and put everything away. Objects were strewn around the room in absolute chaos and disarray, but in front of the camera, things were neat, tidy, and polished.

One thing we can say about ourselves with certainty: we sure know how to get things done on a budget! In our quest to become content creators while spending as little money as possible, some of our shenanigans would have fit in more on an episode of *Extreme Cheapskates.* We actively recommend against you re-creating our DIY setup and potentially setting your home on fire!

In this chapter, we share what we've learned about equipment, including what we recommend you splurge on and where you can cut some corners. We understand that beginner content creators who are just starting out are often operating on tight budgets and still trying to find their niches. That's why we won't advise that you go out and buy the best (and most expensive) thing on the market. Instead, we give you options. Choose the Splurge option if you can afford it! If you're looking to test out some more affordable options before you shell out a ton of cash, choose the Budget option. We love a good hack!

A Good Camera

"I'm filming videos so I need a legit video camera with all the bells and whistles, right?" Not necessarily! We all carry pretty decent cameras in our pockets these days. If you're just getting started, your phone camera is usually more than enough. But if you're ready to level up or want a more cinematic look, investing in a dedicated camera can make sense down the line. You'll get more control over settings like depth of field, focus, and exposure, which can help your content stand out. So should you splurge on something professional and pricey, or just use the camera on your phone? There are pros and cons to each approach.

Splurge: Professional DSLR camera

A professional camera can and will elevate your content! If you are shooting anything visually interesting or beautiful, such as travel content, food, or makeup, a DSLR camera can elevate your videos and help you stand out from other creators who will mostly be using their phones.

Not sure if your content counts as "visually interesting"? Think of it this way: If someone was listening to an audio-only version of your content, podcast style, would the content still be interesting? Or are the visuals a necessary component of the content? That's one way to determine if a quality camera is worth the investment for you.

We had actually been told by a YouTube manager during an introductory meeting that she thought we should upgrade our camera. At first, we were defensive, pointing out that our refurbished DSLR had gotten us to over 200K subscribers! But the more we reflected on her feedback, we realized she was right. We appreciated the fact that she was honest, because she had voiced something that we secretly knew to be true. That was when we made the leap from our old $150 camera to a fancy professional Canon 5D Mark III, and our viewers were wowed. We received so many comments complimenting the upgrade!

How did we choose our camera? We looked at another creator whose content we admired and found a blog post where she discussed what camera she used, and then we purchased the same one. (The creator was haircare entrepreneur and mom blogger Amber Fillerup Clark, in case you were curious!)

If you do choose to buy a camera, we recommend getting one where the screen flips out and you can see yourself while you're filming. Also, don't forget the SD cards!

Budget: Phone camera

If dropping more than a thousand dollars on a professional camera doesn't feel right to you, it's absolutely fine to film and take pictures using the camera on your phone. In fact, we'd recommend starting with your phone for at least the first few months of your content creator journey while you decide if a professional camera is right for you. Particularly if your content is more off the cuff and casual, it's an amazing option. If your content is mostly sitting and talking to the camera, telling stories or sharing your opinions on short-form video, a phone will do just fine because the content is not particularly visually dynamic. Just make sure to bring a phone charger or battery pack with you!

Regularly used by millions of content creators, phones today have excellent filming capabilities. It's just so darn easy and convenient! While a professional camera is heavy and bulky to carry around and requires separate lenses, battery changes, a case, and so on, you simply cannot beat the ease and convenience of pulling your phone out of your pocket and hitting record.

As tempting as it is to just point and shoot, we do recommend optimizing your phone's camera settings and learning to use it effectively. If this is going to be your tool, make the most of it! It'll be worth it to watch a couple of ten-minute tutorials.

Flattering Lighting

Deciding whether to use artificial studio light or natural light is an artistic as well as a practical choice. Good lighting can completely change the mood of your videos, make your setup look polished, your skin tone more even, and your background more intentional. Natural light is great if you're filming near a window or outside, but it can be unpredictable. The sun moves, clouds roll in, and before you know it, your lighting looks totally different halfway through filming. Artificial lighting, on the other hand, gives you consistency and control. Ring lights and softboxes are popular for a reason. They're affordable, adjustable, and easy to use. Whichever one you choose, having inviting lighting will elevate your content.

Splurge: Softbox and ring light

We definitely recommend buying lighting! Lighting makes a huge difference and reduces the amount of editing you have to do later on. Lighting usually isn't very expensive, especially when compared to the cost of a camera. Two softbox lights on Amazon go for $30 to $200, depending on what quality you're looking for. Ring lights can be purchased for even less than that, especially if you get the small portable kind that clip onto your phone, which is perfect for selfie-style talking videos or putting on makeup.

The biggest drawback to using professional lights is that they can be bulky. You'll probably end up leaving them tucked away in a utility closet, in a garage, or just in the corner of your room, depending on how big your living space is. Although they can be a bit of an eyesore, we still think they are absolutely worth it.

Budget: Use natural daylight

If you don't want to use artificial lighting, you can consider using natural lighting. Using natural light can be as much a stylistic choice as it can be a budget-friendly option. Natural sunlight photographs beautifully and can look better than artificial light—it can come off warmer, prettier, and softer, depending on your location and the time of day. It will absolutely take some trial and error to learn the patterns of the sun in your filming location to optimize your content creation best.

The two best times of day for lighting are typically early morning and twilight or dusk. That time in the evening, often known as "golden hour" or "magic hour," is highly sought out by professional photographers. In our home, our living room gets gorgeous light early in the morning. In the evening, the sun has moved to the back of the house. Start to pay attention to the lighting in your filming location. Take some test shots and test video on your phone in different rooms during different times of the day to find the lighting you like best. You're going to want to avoid the midday sun casting harsh shadows on your face. Observing the way the sunlight changes throughout the day can be a game changer when it comes to shooting your content.

Crisp Audio

How perfect does your sound quality need to be? Whether you're speaking to the camera, recording a voiceover, or just adding music to the background, there are some things to consider. Audio can make or break your content. Viewers are surprisingly forgiving of less-than-perfect visuals, but if the sound is muffled, echoey, or full of background noise, they'll tune out fast.

Splurge: Microphone

Microphones can be surprisingly tricky. We've had some great experiences with them, but also plenty of frustrating ones, even with top-quality brands like Rode. There are few things that make you feel more sick to your stomach than spending an entire day filming and then realizing that none of your footage has sound.

If you can get the hang of your microphone and learn how to adjust the settings properly, it can absolutely create a sense of professionalism. Audiences can instantly tell the difference between scratchy, static-filled audio and the crisp, clear sound of a quality mic. If you're making music or singing in your videos, using a microphone isn't optional. It's a must.

Budget: Voiceovers and indoor sound

If you'd rather not use a microphone, there are a few ways to work around it. When speaking directly to the camera, make sure to film indoors where you can control the environment. Try to record in a quiet space with minimal echo. Soft furnishings, curtains, and rugs all help absorb sound. Without a microphone, background noise like cars, birds, or people talking can ruin a video. Shooting indoors can help cut a lot of that out, but you'll still want to make the room as quiet as possible. Turn off anything that hums or buzzes in the background, like air conditioners, dishwashers, washing machines, or fans. Even if it seems quiet to your ears, your camera's microphone will pick it up.

Another option is to record voiceovers directly into your phone or computer. In our experience, both tools tend to have surprisingly good voiceover quality. It's not quite the same as using a professional mic, but it's definitely good enough for most purposes.

You can also make videos that don't include your voice at all, using background music instead. This removes the need to record any audio yourself. That said, this only works for certain types of content.

A Stable Spot for Your Camera

How will you shoot from the best angles no matter where you are? In our opinion, there's an obvious right answer here! A sturdy tripod or stand is one of the most essential pieces of equipment you can own. It keeps your shots steady, your hands free, and your camera safe from accidental tumbles. Stability doesn't just make your videos look more professional; it also lets you focus on your performance instead of worrying about propping your camera on a stack of books.

Splurge: Tripod, phone mount, mirror sticky

We have a lot of experience with haphazard camera setups, so take it from us: just get the tripod! Whether you're using your phone or a camera, it's necessary to have a tripod so you don't just need to hold the phone all the time. Even the most casual, off-the-cuff vlogger needs some sort of camera stand. There are plenty of affordable options available on Amazon. Some mount onto a mirror, which is especially useful when filming for makeup tutorials or "get ready with me" style videos. Others attach to a wall. Some come with bendy wire legs that can adjust to fit a variety of surfaces.

Some tripods come with remote controls and can connect to your phone via Bluetooth so that you can control the camera without having to be within reach of it. It can be overwhelming trying to decide between all the different options. We recommend trying out a few options and returning the items that don't work for you.

Budget: Balance your phone or camera on items you already own

If you'd prefer to skip the tripod or mount, then try balancing your camera on a stack of boxes, books, or folded towels or clothes instead. This tactic can work temporarily, but it's far from ideal. We understand that not everyone wants to invest in equipment right away, but after a few sessions of stacking shoeboxes, readjusting wobbly towers, and trying to keep everything steady every few minutes, you'll quickly realize how much easier life is with a proper stand.

Expert Editing

When you first start out, you're almost surely going to be editing everything yourself. Learning how to cut clips, add captions, and piece your story together is part of the process and helps you understand your own creative rhythm. But as your audience grows, your time may become more limited, and you may wish to look into hiring a pro. A skilled editor can take your raw footage and turn it into something polished, cohesive, and on-brand. Whether you're doing it yourself or outsourcing it to a pro, good editing is what makes your content feel intentional and engaging. It's where all your hard work behind the camera truly comes to life.

Splurge: Hiring an editor

Hiring an editor can free up a huge amount of your time and allow you to focus on what you do best—creating more content. Editing can be tedious, time-consuming, and sometimes frustrating. Having someone else handle it can make your workflow much smoother and let you spend your energy on filming, brainstorming, or engaging with your audience.

There are many ways to find editors. Online platforms such as Upwork and Fiverr make it easy to hire skilled editors remotely, often at competitive rates. You can also hire someone locally through word-of-mouth recommendations from fellow creators or networking events. The right choice depends on your skill level, available time, and budget.

The amount of editing you need to outsource can vary. If your footage requires a lot of cleanup, sending it to a professional will take them a long time and cost more. One suggestion is to do an initial cut yourself, removing long pauses, selecting the best takes, or roughly arranging the clips. Then you can hand it off to a professional for finishing touches, such as adding music, color correction, motion graphics, or other effects. This approach can save money if you are paying your editor by the hour.

Editors may charge by the hour or per project, so it is worth discussing this in advance. Hiring editors from countries such as Mexico, India, or the Philippines can often be more affordable than hiring locally while still providing high-quality work. You can also hire editors for smaller, specific tasks, like creating a ten-second animated intro for your videos. This is a great way to enhance your content without committing to full-scale editing.

Budget: Editing software or free editing apps

When we first started our channel, we would easily spend hours editing a single minute of footage. Over the years, we often discussed hiring an editor, but as time went on, we got faster and better at editing ourselves. Eventually, we became so good at it that we decided hiring someone would be an unnecessary expense.

The alternative to hiring an editor is doing it yourself using editing software. When we first started out, we used iMovie because it was free and already installed on our Mac laptop. Windows Movie Maker came free with the purchase of our Dell laptop.

Eventually we each purchased Final Cut Pro X. But honestly, we don't recommend paying for editing software. We found that the free software worked just as well. Upgrading our camera made a bigger impact on our final product.

There are many free and low-cost editing apps you can use directly on your phone, such as InShot and CapCut. Find what works best for you.

It's worth noting that video footage takes up a huge amount of storage space, especially if you are shooting in high definition or 4K. Even a few minutes of raw footage can quickly eat up several gigabytes, and when you start accumulating multiple projects, your laptop's internal storage can fill up fast. For this reason, if you plan to edit on a laptop, investing in external hard drives is almost essential. Having a reliable storage setup ensures you can work efficiently without constantly worrying about running out of space or losing valuable footage.

Filming Locations

Do you shoot at home, in public spaces, in a rented studio, or some combination of all of these places? Each option offers positives and negatives. Filming at home is convenient and cost-effective. You can set your schedule, control your environment, and avoid rental fees. Public spaces can add energy, authenticity, and variety to your videos. Shooting outdoors or in dynamic locations like cafés, parks, or city streets can make your content more visually engaging. Rented studios offer full control over lighting, sound, and backgrounds, making them ideal for projects that require a polished, professional look.

Splurge: Rent a studio space

Renting a studio space or nice Airbnb can be an awesome idea, especially if you are filming specialized content. For example, if you create cooking videos, you might want to film in a nice kitchen.

The obvious drawback is that these spaces can be very expensive. Often billed by the hour, with a minimum number of hours, this option will cost hundreds, thousands, or even tens of thousands of dollars, depending on where you're renting and for how long. Although shooting in a professional rented space can garner beautiful results, it's more pricey and less practical. Most creators shoot either in their homes or public spaces.

If you do rent a space, you're going to want to maximize your time there and really get your money's worth. Wherever and however you choose to film, whether it's at home or in a rented studio space, it's always more efficient to batch your content. This just means you're going to shoot lots of content at once—either lots of videos or lots of clips of videos that you can weave together. Batching your content requires planning in advance so you don't waste time in your rented space. Melissa Tierney, a content creator known by the handle @MissyOnMadison who combines her love of fashion with her passion for all things Disney, says, "For me, what's easiest is just taking certain days that are just content creation days and batching it. The last time I was at Disney World was a year ago, but you would never know that by looking at my content. I plan all my outfits, rent a stroller to push them around, shoot my content for a few days. That gives me plenty of content for months to come!"

Budget: Use your home or public spaces

Filming inside your home is obviously the most convenient (not to mention free!) option. But not everyone is fortunate enough to live in a camera-worthy space.

When we started our social media journey, we lived with our parents, who were hoarders. Yes, you read that correctly—hoarders. So filming at our home was a struggle. Just getting a plain white wall as our background involved hours of moving furniture, scrubbing down the wall, and so on. We had one single spot in the house to film sit-and-talks, and that was Shanna's bedroom. Because that room was under her domain, it wasn't filled with stuff our parents were hoarding, and she set it up so it would look nice on camera. We dreaded filming sponsored outfit videos because those required full-body camera shots where, unlike our typical close-up shots from the shoulders up, more of the room's background needed to be visible. Those shots required far more clean wall space than we had access to in Shanna's small bedroom, and we quickly learned that our house was simply not a place we could capture quality content like that. Brands that were paying us thousands of dollars to showcase their clothing wanted to see those outfits in a clean, attractive, welcoming environment, not a cluttered, dingy hoarder house.

Marissa attended a local university, California State University, Northridge. It has a beautiful campus with plenty of good backgrounds, so that became our go-to spot for filming our videos. We loved the opportunity to get creative with locations, often walking around campus finding interesting backgrounds, like a brick wall or a cluster of orange trees, for our outfits or to shoot scenes for our skits.

We'd also bring different outfits to switch things up so our scenes would look more complex and like they had been shot over the course of several days. We particularly liked wearing jackets, hats, and scarves because they can completely change the look of an outfit and didn't require us to find a bathroom to change in.

We've also shot in other public spaces, like malls, movie theaters, and restaurants. It can be tricky to know when to ask permission and when not to ask permission. If there's a small business you'd like to shoot in, definitely ask permission! If they have a social media presence they update regularly, then you can bet that they care about social media marketing. This means they will be more likely to grant permission in exchange for some promotion.

If you're nervous to film in a public space—you may get some funny looks—but don't have another option, we recommend shooting quickly and discreetly. Prior prep work is key! You may want to do a prior visit to figure out where exactly you want to film. Then swoop in, get it done, and get the heck out of there.

If someone approaches you while you're filming and asks you to stop, then you should absolutely respect their request and stop filming. You always want to be respectful of those around you, especially when filming in a business like a store or a movie theater. If they ask you to stop, you can always go find another location.

A final reminder is to try to take advantage of any extraordinary or unique locations you happen to come across, even if it doesn't fit into your regular content. If you're going to be traveling to an exotic destination, attending a wedding, or visiting someplace visually interesting like a zoo, theme park, or a particularly stunning hotel, try to think of some content you can shoot there to capitalize on the uniqueness of the location. Keep an eye out for anything visually spectacular or unusual.

5

Networking Basics

For having the word "social" in it, social media can often feel like a decidedly solitary and isolating experience. Much of the work unfolds within the confines of your home or with a limited circle of associates.

The art of networking in the digital era, both in person and online, is an often underutilized skill that can give you a competitive advantage over other influencers.

In this chapter, we clue you in to how the transformative potential of networking can maximize your opportunities on social media.

Making Friends with Other Creators

The best way to grow in the creator space is to put yourself out there. One introduction can lead to another, and before you know it, you're surrounded by like-minded people who understand your journey.

Positivity is contagious, so spread it generously! When you come across a video you like, don't just scroll by; leave a thoughtful comment. When someone shares something thought-provoking or vulnerable on their IG stories, send a supportive message their way. Compliments are free, and kindness with no agenda goes a long way.

Befriending other creators comes with incredible benefits:

- **Genuine friendships.** You'll meet people who truly get what it's like to be a creator: the highs, the lows, and everything in between.
- **Expanded network.** Knowing one creator often means getting introduced to others. Creators tend to support and collaborate with each other.
- **Collaborations and growth.** Cross-promotions, shoutouts, and collaborations can introduce you to new audiences. (We cover this topic in depth in chapter 6.)
- **Industry insights.** Stay in the loop with algorithm changes, growth strategies, and brand partnership tips by engaging with others in the field.
- **Brand contacts and opportunities.** While sharing brand rates and insider info requires discretion, knowing the right people can open doors to better opportunities.

In-person Events

Events, like new product launches, brand parties, and content creator conferences such as VidCon can offer incredible benefits, but they can also be intimidating and trigger social anxiety. Many creators are introverted or feel nervous transitioning from online interactions to real-life conversations. Being comfortable alone in front of a camera doesn't always translate to confidence in real-life interactions. In fact, creators with massive followings are often some of the most insecure and anxious people in social settings. If social anxiety makes networking feel overwhelming, here are some strategies to help you socialize at in-person events.

Small-talk tips

Set a goal of starting just one or two low-stakes conversations. Practice small talk before the event. You could comment on the food, music, or décor. You could compliment the other person's outfit or makeup, especially if you can tell they put a lot of effort into it.

Be careful not to complain or say anything negative. We once made the mistake of trying to connect with some other creators by commiserating about how late the party was starting. The other creators just smiled awkwardly at us, looking uncomfortable. We then understood that they weren't responding because they didn't want to bad-mouth the brand that invited us. We ended up feeling a little embarrassed, like they thought we were baiting them into saying something unprofessional.

Try to either keep the conversation light and positive or just ask people basic questions about themselves. For example, you could ask them about the kind of content they make, or if they are from the city where the event is being held, or if they had to travel. Mention something about yourself that they can comment on or ask you about, such as an interesting hobby you have, a trip you took, or a movie you saw. Don't be afraid to share things about yourself and open up. Skip the trauma dumping, though! And always remember to smile. A smile changes your whole face and instantly communicates friendliness.

Say hello to the person who invited you

When you give your name at the check-in table, inquire about the person whose name was on the invitation emails. Just say, "Hi, I was invited by First Name, Last Name, who works at X. Do you know where they are so I can say hi?" They might know, they might not. The person you ask might even be the same person who invited you! It's always nice to connect with them in person and put a face to a name. You can also sneakily look up their photo on LinkedIn and look around for them. It's a great way to make a personal connection and stay on their radar for future events!

Bring a plus-one

Some events will allow you to bring a plus-one, such as a friend or spouse. There are pros and cons to this. First of all, it's super helpful to have an extra person there to take content of you. Without a plus-one, you're left asking strangers to take picture or videos of you, which can be hit or miss. Nothing ruins a killer photo op like a blurry shot with someone's thumb in the frame. A plus-one can also assist with practical tasks, like holding your purse or jacket while you pose, carrying heavy gift bags to the car, or helping share the cost of parking or valet. Beyond the logistics, having a familiar face nearby can make you feel calmer and more confident in what can be an intimidating environment.

On the other hand, attending alone can be beneficial, too. Going solo encourages you to step out of your comfort zone and meet new people. If you go with a friend, there is a risk you might spend the entire event talking to them and not getting to know anybody else.

The best of both worlds is going with another content creator who is invited to the same event. This requires going to at least one in-person event where you can get the ball rolling and meet a few people. Then, you can arrange to attend future events together. If there's an event that pops up that your creator friend isn't invited to, you can always ask the event organizer if you can invite the other creator as your plus-one.

(Brands generally love getting double the exposure that way!) Try to find someone who lives close by so you can carpool together. The advantage of this is that you each have a social circle, and by teaming up, you can expand each other's reach.

Sharing Contacts and Rates

One of the benefits of in-person networking and making friends with other content creators is the ability to share valuable information with others. However, there is a right way and a wrong way to go about this. Doing this the right way can strengthen relationships and build trust, but done poorly, it can feel awkward or even off-putting. Remember, the goal is to help each other, not to compete or create tension.

People can be very private and protective of their contacts, particularly for paid deals. That's because they are valuable, hard to track down, hard to cultivate, and hard to maintain. Brand employees also switch positions frequently, so having updated contact information is difficult to come by. Some entrepreneurial influencers even sell curated lists of PR brand contacts for hundreds of dollars.

No one wants to feel like they're being used, or like you're faking an interest in them just to ask for favors or poach their valuable contacts. So if you're asking someone for a valuable contact, you absolutely *must* make it mutually beneficial! We cannot stress this enough!

We remember a time we approached another content creator at a YouTube Space event. We had met her a few times previously at other events and we were on friendly terms. We saw that she had just worked with a popular clothing brand that we were dying to work with. We worked up the courage and asked her for the email, and in the same breath we told her we could send her contact information for anyone we had recently worked with, promptly listing off several trendy makeup brands we had worked with on both paid and unpaid deals. We remember we didn't even pause between asking her for the favor and offering to reciprocate because we were so worried we'd offend her.

She paused a moment, taking in what we had just said. She then brightly agreed to give us the contact email, mentioning that she already had some of the makeup contacts we were offering, but that she had seen us work with a different makeup brand that she wanted to try. We happily traded contacts. The email contact she gave us was for a very specific person at a PR agency that we had never heard of before. We never, ever would have been able to find it on our own through creative googling! Long story short, we ended up booking several lucrative deals with the clothing company—two campaigns that totaled around $30,000!

We were so grateful that we'd had the courage to ask for the contact info, because that connection paid off in a big way. If we hadn't offered up our own contacts in exchange, she might not have agreed to share hers. If done wrong, the exchange could have ended our friendship altogether. Maybe you don't have any valuable brand contacts to offer up, but you're great at editing videos, taking headshots, or graphic design. Other creators can be a valuable resource, but you've got to offer something if you want something.

Remember, everyone's nervous. You're not alone in feeling this way. Putting yourself out there can be scary, but the right connections can make your journey as a creator so much more fulfilling. Take the leap. You never know who you might meet.

Connecting with Brands, Agencies, and Local Functions

First, focus on events in your local city or the closest big city to you. We find that small, local events are some of the easiest to get in with, particularly with seasonal, holiday-based activations, such as Christmas,

Halloween, New Years, or Easter. They are typically looking for positive press to help drive ticket sales for these limited-time events.

Look up local events. Go to the event's website and search for a section for "press/media." Guess what, that's you! You're press/media! Press does not just mean major outlets like CNN or *The New York Times*; it means small local media like you! You will typically have to fill out a form with details about your publication, the audience it reaches, and the audience's demographics. You want to give professional answers. For example, we say that our audience is "aged eighteen- to thirty-four-year-old, US-based females." This gives the event organizer an idea of who they can expect us to reach.

You also should explain how you plan on featuring the event. This sounds obvious, but it's something most people don't do. For example, let them know that you're going to do Instagram stories, a Facebook Post, or a TikTok video, or that you're going to recap the event for your email subscribers and offer them a discount code on tickets. Describe what the content will look like. The more specific you can be, the better.

The next thing you want to do is email local PR agencies. You'll need to do some research. Once you find an agency, check out their Instagram page so that you can look for events, activations, and brands that the agency already works with that you're interested in. This way, when you contact them, you can ask for something ultra specific, such as "I'd love to attend opening night of the such-and-such annual spooky haunted house and feature the event on my channel!" This is much more effective than a generic outreach email that asks to be considered for anything and everything.

Know your value

It's important that you don't get intimidated. Don't assume that your audience is too small, or too niche, or that what you have to offer isn't good enough. If you do, you are counting yourself out before you even get started. Remember, by reaching out and explicitly explaining how you'll promote the event, you are making these peoples' jobs easy. The worst thing they can say is no.

Remember, even if your audience may seem small, many brands hire special social media, PR, and brand managers specifically for content. They pay them a salary, sometimes over six figures, for the production and distribution of content. Here you are, an individual willing to trade in valuable content in exchange for goods and services. Do not undervalue that.

Traveling for Events

Samuel Bennett is a photographer who creates sports content primarily about paintball. He's based in Tampa, Florida, and has this to say about traveling for events: "I've flown all around the country. Typically, I will go to Los Angeles or New York or, more recently, Atlanta. I wanted to fly out because I knew that the opportunities to meet other creators just weren't really there in Tampa, at least not like these other places. So for me, it is worth it to head out to meet them and become friends with a lot of them. It's truly been an honor to do it, and I would never take back anything I've done. I do think it was well worth it for what I wanted to do in the creator space."

If you live in a major city like LA, New York, Chicago, or Nashville, you probably have access to a plethora of events. But if you live in a small town like Spearfish, South Dakota (or even Tampa, Florida), you'll probably have to do some traveling. It's up to you to decide if the event is worth the trip. Unfortunately, there's no way of knowing whether an event is going to be a bust or not until you go!

Here are some questions you may want to ask yourself when deciding whether to spend your valuable time, energy, and money attending a networking event:

What are the posting obligations for attending this event? Are you required to post about it? Are you required to do a certain number of posts? Do the posts need to be approved by someone beforehand, or will you be free to post what you want, when you want, at your discretion? You really should post about the event, and, of course, the brand hopes you will, but it's different when there's an obligation with a deadline or a contract.

Will there be monetary compensation for attending and posting about the event? For example, will you be paid to post an Instagram story from the event? This is rare, but it definitely can happen! Toyota paid us to attend the LA Auto Show and post about their newest car.

Will you be compensated with the company's products? We've had some clothing brands such as Forever 21, Pretty Little Thing, Revolve, JCPenney, Victoria's Secret PINK, American Eagle Outfitters, and BooHoo offer us gift cards in exchange for attending their event or posting about their products.

Is this event open to the general public, or is it a private event? If the event is open to the general public, will there be a private area for talent, or any special perks for talent (free tickets, front-of-the-line pass, free food voucher)?

Is this an event you can pay to do on your own or is this an experience that money typically can't buy? Experiences that fall into this category include a private meet and greet with a band, getting to visit a theme park after hours, or getting to skip the lines.

Will there be food and beverages and/or alcohol provided?

Will there be entertainment?

Will there be a gift bag or free swag? Will you be one of the people receiving the gift bag or will it only go to select people?

Will it cost money to attend this event? Will you have to purchase your own ticket, even as a creator?

Will transportation be provided for you to and from the event, or will you have to pay for your own transportation? This could be anything from paying for your own plane ticket and hotel room, to paying for your own ridesharing car, to paying for your own parking.

Will there be a red carpet? Will you be able to walk on the red carpet as talent?

Will there be professional photographers? Is your photo likely to end up on an editorial news website like Getty Images? For some people, having their photo on Getty Images adds credibility and legitimacy to their position as a content creator or is considered "clout."

Will there be opportunities to do media interviews or PR opportunities? You may want to consider hiring a publicist for major red-carpet events to make the most of it!

Will there be other talent you can mingle with? We're not just talking about other content creators, but actors, singers, or models.

Will there be business professionals you can mingle with, in addition to the brand or organization that invited you?

Has the brand or organization that invited you done a paid deal with you in the past? Has the brand ever sent you their products before? We like to support brands that have worked with us before.

Could there be an opportunity to do a paid deal with this brand in the future? Some brands simply don't pay influencers, either because it doesn't align with their marketing strategy, or because they don't have the budget. Does this brand have a history of doing *paid* deals with creators or is free gifting the best you can hope for?

Will you have fun, or will this feel like work?

Will you learn something valuable at the event?

If you skip this event, will you have "FOMO" (fear of missing out)? Is there something else you would rather be doing?

There are no right or wrong answers to any of these questions. We're not in any way suggesting that you should only attend events that pay you to attend, let you walk on red carpets, or offer free alcohol! These are merely food-for-thought questions you may want to consider when deciding whether or not an event is worth your time and money. We are all leading busy lives with obligations to our friends, family, and careers. It's good to be selective so that you can zero in on what you hope to get out of these events and stay focused on your long-term goals.

Making the Most of Every Event

Once you're at the event, you'll want to make the most of your experience. Here are some things to keep in mind while you're out having fun and representing your personal brand.

Your celebrity persona: Develop a signature look

With in-person events, make sure you make an effort and dress up. It sounds superficial, but dressing nicely will make you seem more approachable and friendly.

The first year we went to Beautycon, which was a major beauty convention where creators, brands, and fans all mingled in a large space, we both wore a simple t-shirt and jeans. Not many people approached or chatted with us. The next year, we put a lot more effort into our outfits and wore complementing pink and yellow dresses that were bright, sunny, and glam. The difference was night and day! So many people approached us that year! The event even posted a static IG picture of us on the pink carpet in front of their step-and-repeat media backdrop.

At events, people don't have a lot to go on, so give them a reason to approach you. One way to be more approachable is by making your outfit a conversation starter! That's why we like to deliberately wear at least one attention-grabbing statement piece.

Remember, this is not a corporate event where everyone is in a suit and tie. You're among creatives! Have some fun with it.

We also believe that if you are physically comfortable, you will have a better overall experience. Always dress for the weather and wear comfortable shoes! If you're going to wear high heels, make sure you can walk in them. Consider bringing a change of shoes. We've done that for movie premieres and gotten Getty Images pictures taken on the red carpet in our nice shoes, then switched to our comfy flats as soon as we entered the lobby. The only downside to this is that you have to bring a bag large enough to hold an extra pair of shoes.

Monitor your social battery

Remember that you aren't obligated to stay for the entire event, especially if it goes on late into the night or you aren't enjoying yourself. If you are having an amazing time and want to stay until the end, then go ahead, but you don't have to. Some creators do "event-hopping," flitting around the city from one event to another, typically during particularly busy seasons like Fashion Week, Festival Season, and the winter holidays. While some creators love cramming in every single event they can fit into their schedule, others, like us, can find it absolutely exhausting. You already have a lot going on with handling administrative work like emails, editing, scheduling content, and—oh yeah—creating content! So don't spread yourself so thin that you're unable to keep up with your business.

Stay classy

Some networking and creator events have an open bar, and as tempting as it is to go wild and take advantage of the free drinks, limit yourself. Always remember this is still a professional event. It's sort of the equivalent of getting wasted at the company holiday party, except when you're with content creators, you're among a gossipy group of people with influence across the internet. Not to mention, the party is obviously being hosted by a brand, a company, or an organization that you want to impress.

If it turns out to be a boring event, save your critiques for the privacy of your own home at the end of the night. Try to refrain from posting any complaints on your social media. What will complaining do for you? Try to roll with the punches. The party starts late? They run out of gift bags? Someone is rude to you? Privately, you may be seething. Privately, you may be enraged. But what is an angry post going to do for you in the long run? Not a whole lot. Is it going to help your career? No. All it's going to do is ensure that the brand will take you off their PR list and never invite you to one of their events again, and other brands will be wary of working with you. They'll see you as not "brand safe" and won't want to associate with you. Instead of being overly negative and critical about it, you can choose not to post about the event.

6

Collaborating with Creators

Some of the most effective ways to reach new audiences and create fresh content can be through collaborations with other creators. Some of the advantages are that you'll be able to reach a new and eager audience, gain followers, and perhaps even make a close connection in the industry.

However, collaborations aren't without challenges. You might end up facing backlash or hate from the other creator's followers. The other creator could be rude or unreliable. You could put in the work and successfully finish the collab, but not see any growth.

In this chapter, we explain what collaborations really do and don't do for a creator's growth. Collaborations work best when they are treated as a brand-building opportunity rather than a shortcut to huge surges in followers. You'll learn how to approach creators respectfully, how to build rapport without seeming opportunistic, and how to decide whether a potential partnership is worth the time, travel, or emotional energy. Collaborations can also come with personality clashes, mismatched levels of professionalism, and broken promises that turn a simple video idea into a stressful experience. But don't panic; we'll help you protect your time, mental health, and boundaries.

Growth Isn't Guaranteed

The biggest misconception about collaborations is the impact they will have. When asking other influencers and industry professionals how many new viewers they think a collab would yield, we have heard a wide variety of answers. "At least 5 to 10 percent of the other creator's audience size," said one person. "You can easily earn 5,000 new viewers if you did one new collab a month," one digital professional boasted. But the cold, hard truth is that the impact is far less than you would imagine. People tend to vastly overestimate the number of followers they'll gain from a collab, even if that collab is with an account that has a huge following.

When PewDiePie featured our channel in a video, he was the largest creator on YouTube with more than 50 million followers. Guess how many new subscribers we earned from it? Well, according to the person who said 5 to 10 percent of their audience size, we should've gotten at least 2.5 million new fans. We'll give you a hint: it was nowhere close to that. In total, we gained a little less than 5,000 new followers. It was, undoubtedly, a significant boost, but nowhere close to what you would think a channel of that size and popularity would bring. When Shane Dawson, another prominent creator at the time, mentioned us in several videos, the first time we attracted about 3,000 new subscribers. The second time he mentioned us, we got a modest 1,500 new subs.

Regardless of whether the creator is larger or smaller, managing expectations is also key. Don't go into a collab with someone who has 100K followers thinking you're going to end up with 10K new followers.

This kind of growth is possible, depending on the person's engagement and how viral the content may go, but you shouldn't anticipate it. That's the disappointing answer that no one wants to hear, but it's the truth. Most of your growth will ultimately come from you implementing other strategies, but that's not to say you can't get a much-needed boost from a collab. Working with the right creator can also make your own brand more appealing. Partnering with a respected figure in your niche can strengthen your personal brand and position you as a peer in that space. For example, if you want to establish yourself as an expert in DIY home renovation, collaborating with well-known home renovation creators can help potential partners see you as part of the same professional category, opening doors to new opportunities.

The Power of Partnerships

To be honest, collabs are very hit or miss. Creators can be a delight to film with or an absolute nightmare. It can make for fun, dynamic, and interesting content . . . or a cautionary tale to share with others. Of course, it's better to form an organic connection with a creator, because this will translate better throughout the content, which may limit you to creators in your surrounding area and people you can meet up with and film with in person.

For example, in the Beauty/Lifestyle realm, two creators that exemplify making their friendship an integral part of their brand are Alisha Marie and Remi Ashten. They share a popular podcast together called *Pretty Basic*, but even going back over a decade ago they would make appearances together at events and do branded campaigns together. It seemed to be a very strategic and effective way to combine internet empires together. Let us get really millennial right about now and ask you to think of the band the Spice Girls. How many songs can you name? Probably at least a few of the popular ones. Now if we were to ask you to name songs from the solo albums of Melanie C, Melanie B, Emma Bunton, Victoria Beckham, and Geri Halliwell, how many could you name? Our guess would be not as many. By joining forces as a band, they created a much deeper and richer result than they might have had as solo creators.

That being said, even one-off collabs with creators in town for events like VidCon, for example, can be very impactful. Realistically, you're not going to gel and become BFFs with every single creator you collab with, and that's okay. The point is to create a mutually beneficial opportunity for both parties.

Approaching a Collab

It's all well and good to emphasize creating friendships with influencers and collaborating in a meaningful way, but how do you go about doing that in a way that doesn't seem calculated and opportunistic?

After all, depending on where you are, it's not always ideal to just say "meet them at events." Events in your area can be great for networking, but let's say you stumble across a creator with whom you think you'd make fun content. Being proactive and making the first move is important. Make sure to follow them, as it's pretty awkward when someone who's "a huge fan and would love to collab" isn't even following you. Also, as a general rule of thumb, it's good to engage with their content—liking, commenting, and even DMing them or responding to stories. (We're using Instagram and TikTok as an example of how to create a rapport, since it's far harder to contact someone via YouTube.) Or if you'll be visiting their city, you can ask to meet up with them.

It's important to be professional with someone you're trying to collab with for the first time because this person isn't your friend yet. Be polite and on time. You can discuss other influencers, but avoid bashing anyone. This industry is smaller than you might think, and gossip can travel quickly.

The Collab from Hell

Unfortunately, bad collabs are inevitable, especially as you participate in more and more of them. We once worked with a DIY and creative arts and crafts influencer whom we'll refer to as HannaBanana100 for the purposes of this example. HannaBanana100 asked her manager to reach out to us to see if we'd like to film a collab video. We'd spoken to her a few times at events, followed each other, and interacted here and there, so, naturally, we agreed to her request to collaborate even though we were the larger channel at the time by a significant amount. We weren't close friends with her but had seen her enough times and were decent enough acquaintances where it seemed like it could be a good idea.

Not even close.

We set up a date and time to film together. We traveled by Uber for over an hour to go to her apartment across town to film the collab. We brought our camera and tripod and had pre-planned the video concepts. We planned on shooting two videos with her: one video to go live on her channel, and one video to go live on our channel. Our goal was to provide some more engaging content for our audience, create a break from our usual videos, and ultimately boost each other's follower count.

The day we filmed the videos, our interaction with HannaBanana100 was pretty ordinary. She was polite, pleasant, and relatively efficient. We filmed both videos in a few hours, and it seemed by all counts that everything was going well. We made small talk with her about living in LA, mutual friends in the industry, and our favorite restaurants. Afterward, the three of us took an Uber together to a party hosted by the fashion company BooHoo. She didn't help pay for the Uber, and that was just the beginning.

We had previously agreed that the collabs would go live in two weeks so we could have a chance to properly edit them and to make the thumbnails, descriptions, and tags for the videos. The date we agreed on came, and we posted our half of the project, urging people to go and follow her and check out the video we did on her channel. But when we checked her channel, we noticed that she hadn't uploaded the other video.

So we texted her, thinking that maybe she'd forgotten the date and this was all just an honest mistake. She responded, saying that she had another collab going live the next day and she didn't want to post ours right before her other collabs. This seemed like a very bizarre excuse, but we said okay and asked when she would post her portion of the project, since ours had already been live for a while. No answer.

The days went by and HannaBanana100 got a nice little boost of around 4,000 new followers, which pushed her over the 300K subscriber mark. She began posting collabs with other creators, but she still didn't post the video we all worked on together. We texted her again and asked about our collab. Again, no response. At that point we got the feeling that she was planning to ghost us. After at least a month had gone by, we reached out to her manager as a last resort and asked about the collaboration. After all, we'd done all the work and put forth effort into going across town to film with her, editing, posting, and so on. The least she could do is post it even if it's late, right? Her manager was incredibly kind and apologetic and seemed embarrassed by her client's behavior.

The next day, we finally received a text from HannahBanana100, and it wasn't what either one of us expected.

> "How dare you reach out to my manager like that! Maybe I didn't want to post the collab because I didn't like the way I looked in it. Some people have issues like that, and you should really think about that before being so rude and insensitive. I won't be posting the collab, but I'll shout you out in a future video . . . but I'll just have a bad taste in my mouth when I do it."

Needless to say, we were shocked and horrified by her answer. The future shoutout she promised? It never materialized. Rather than following up with her or her manager, we decided to let it go. We never heard from her again, and thank goodness for that. One valuable lesson we learned from all of this was that not every collab will be a success. There will be some collabs where you really hit it off with the other creator but don't generate any new audience members. There will be other collabs where you don't really click with the creator, and you know intuitively that you won't be collaborating again, but the content goes viral, and you earn a bunch of new viewers. But the most frustrating scenario, which is rare but does indeed happen, is spending time and effort shooting content that will never see the light of day.

Thankfully, out of all of our less-than-ideal collabs, we've never had a repeat of anything quite like that, but at least we could find solace in knowing that we learned a lot from our experience with HannaBanana100, including how to manage collaborations in the future.

Go the Extra Mile to Make the Collab a Success

If you're reaching out to someone to try to collaborate, even something as simple as offering to go to their side of town or hanging out first and getting lunch before filming can make all the difference.

Being overly accommodating is not always a good thing, but it can certainly work out well in the right context. For example, years ago, we did several YouTube collaborations with Nia Sioux, who'd been one of the original girls on the hit Lifetime show called *Dance Moms*. We'd met her at a premiere for the movie *Alice Through the Looking Glass* and became fast friends.

She'd just started a YouTube channel and had a few videos posted, but nothing really capitalizing off the success of *Dance Moms*, which was still ongoing and filming new seasons in LA. We suggested a fun collab where we pretended to prank call dance instructor Abby Lee Miller. (Plot twist: we didn't actually do it, although we did prank call her costar JoJo Siwa!) We offered to edit the video for her and make the thumbnail because she didn't have as much experience with content creation. It took us hours, but we are glad we volunteered to do the work because the collab was a massive success. The video on her channel yielded just under 4 million views, and over 500K views on ours! It ended up being well worth it to go above and beyond for our collaborator. Collabs should be mutually beneficial for both parties.

Successes and Failures

Over the course of our digital careers, we've been part of collaborations that went really well and others that didn't. Most of the time, it's not as simple as calling one good and another bad. A lot of collabs have a mix of both. That said, most will lean in one direction. They'll either feel successful or not, worth it or not. Stay open to the idea of working with someone again, but trust your instincts. Sometimes, it's just not a smart use of your time, energy, money, or creative bandwidth to team up with certain influencers.

Prioritizing Your Safety

When an online interaction moves into real life, it's crucial to remember that people aren't always who they appear to be behind their carefully curated personas. A friendly DM asking to collab doesn't guarantee that someone's intentions are genuine. Collaborations can open doors to amazing opportunities, but they can also come with risks. Always prioritize your well-being and security above all else to ensure your collaboration is productive and safe.

Back in the summer of 2015, we attended Beautycon in downtown Los Angeles, a buzzing festival for beauty enthusiasts and creators. The convention center was packed with booths, product launches, and endless photo ops. For content creators, it was a rare chance to network and connect in person with others in the community.

But one brief exchange that day left a lasting impression, although we wouldn't understand its significance until many years later.

In the VIP lounge, a group of us young female creators were chatting when Shanna struck up a conversation with a friendly redheaded girl. Shanna complimented her striking Instagram profile photo—a vivid rooftop shot against a bright blue sky.

"That's such a beautiful picture!" Shanna exclaimed. "Did you take it yourself, or did a photographer shoot it?"

"A photographer," the redheaded girl replied casually.

"Who's the photographer?" Shanna asked, eager to find someone who could take new photos for our channel.

Her demeanor instantly shifted. She looked down and changed the subject. When we said goodbye a few minutes later, Shanna tried again, asking directly for the photographer's name and contact information.

This time, she looked visibly upset. "No," she said sharply. "I can't tell you. Please, just trust me. I can't tell you who, and I can't tell you why."

Shanna walked away, annoyed, assuming this girl was being a gatekeeper about her industry connections.

Seven years later, in 2022, Shanna came across a name she didn't recognize: Kaalan Walker. He had been sentenced to fifty years to life in prison for multiple counts of sexual assault. He had allegedly lured aspiring models and creators into photoshoots by promising them fake professional opportunities.

Shanna scrolled through Instagram one evening and saw a post from the same redheaded girl she'd met at Beautycon, still a content creator.

She shared those same photos Shanna had admired years earlier—the ones taken on the rooftop. In her caption, she revealed that the photographer was Kaalan Walker and that she was one of his victims. She wrote that she had kept that photo as her profile picture all these years as a small act of reclamation, a way to take back power from an experience that had stolen so much.

Her refusal to share his name all those years ago wasn't gatekeeping. It was protection. That realization has stayed with us. Even when someone seems genuine, well-known, or trustworthy, their reputation can mask danger. Predators often hide behind charm, status, and social credibility.

If you're ever meeting up with someone you met online for a collaboration, prioritize your safety. Never go alone. Bring a friend, partner, or parent. Let others know exactly where you'll be and when you plan to return. Keep your phone's location sharing on. Avoid drinking or using substances around someone you've just met. When possible, meet in a public place, like a coffee shop, park, or rented studio space. No matter how familiar someone may seem online, remember that what you see on a screen is only an image, not a guarantee of who they truly are.

PART 2

Dealing with Challenges

7

Setting Your Boundaries

The days of a select few top influencers dominating each platform are long gone, replaced by a multitude of influencers vying for recognition. Getting attention online feels a bit like *The Hunger Games*, a dog-eat-dog battle to the death. It's a battlefield of influencers struggling for acknowledgment for being the "realest" by constantly oversharing, and so the line of personal boundaries is more blurred than ever before.

In a world teeming with social media stars, the pursuit of attention raises some philosophical questions: What are you comfortable with? What are you not comfortable with? What pushes the boundaries of your comfort zone? What ignites your passion? What sends shivers down your spine? And where do you want to draw the line?

In this era, nearly everyone, whether an influencer or not, leaves behind a digital footprint. It's not impossible to change your digital footprint later down the road, but doing so poses significant challenges. Remember, the internet isn't written in pencil; it's written in pen. By instilling strong boundaries early in your digital era, you minimize unintended backlash and issues in your personal and professional life. You want your social media presence to become an asset rather than an unintended liability. The way you choose to show up online helps shape your story as a creator.

Finding a Balance

Social media boundaries can be a hotly debated topic. Some creators feel strongly about only posting curated and informational content. Others value the authenticity of sharing personal information about their views and experiences.

The key takeaway is to find the balance that works for you and share what you feel comfortable with. Your comfort level may also change throughout your journey. There might be days when you feel like being more candid and vulnerable with your audience and days when you just want to stick with some curated content.

The ultimate goal is to create strong relationships with your audience that make them feel connected to you and keep them coming back to consume your content on a regular basis. Parasocial relationships are one-sided connections where individuals invest emotional energy, time, and interest in a persona without the influencer being aware of their existence. Influencers, by virtue of their curated online personas, often find themselves fostering these connections with their followers. Through consistent content sharing, genuine engagement, and relatable narratives, influencers create an illusion of intimacy, leading followers to develop a sense of connection and familiarity.

Understanding the intricacies of parasocial relationships is pivotal for influencers as they navigate the fine line between genuine connection and the curated nature of their online presence. Successful influencers leverage this unique bond to establish a loyal audience, recognizing that the power of parasocial relationships extends beyond mere follower counts to create a community that resonates on a personal level.

Deciding What to Share (and What to Keep Private)

In today's social media landscape, the term "authenticity" echoes through the corridors of the influencer world, a buzzword laden with complexity.

What does it mean to be truly authentic online? Is it necessary to share everything about yourself to be authentic? If someone asks you a question, are you required to answer with unfiltered transparency? Do you need to post about your bad days, your tears, and your worst moments to escape the dreaded accusation of "only posting a highlight reel"? Is it essential to overshare to be considered authentic?

Your online canvas is yours to paint, and the brushstrokes can reflect your unique version of authenticity, without the need to breach personal boundaries. Craft an online presence that resonates with your genuine self, steering clear of compromising your comfort for the elusive pursuit of authenticity.

Let's explore the nitty-gritty decisions that will mold your digital presence.

Moniker matters: Legal versus pseudonym

Will your social media account proudly display your legal first and last name, or will you adopt a pseudonym for a touch of mystique? The choice may hinge on privacy concerns or the allure of a catchy alias.

Pros of using your real name can include boosting name recognition and creating a stronger, more authentic brand. However, this can create privacy issues, as your audiences will have easy access to your personal information.

If you decide to use a pseudonym, keep in mind that you should choose a name that you wouldn't mind growing with. Say you start posting successful young adult content under the name SparklePuppyXO19, but then decide you want to switch up your content and post about a more serious topic, such as financial advice. That might be a difficult transition to make because viewers probably won't take you seriously with a name like "SparklePuppyXO19."

You might also want to use a pseudonym if your real name isn't easy to pronounce. Los Angeles–based beauty and fashion creator whose real first name is Liraz says, "I go by Glam by Roxy mainly because people don't know how to pronounce my name, but not for security purposes."

We both chose to use our real first names, but we swapped our last names for our middle names. Our actual last name is tough to pronounce and so uncommon that it's way too easy for people to dig up personal details about us. Keeping it off the internet adds a small but meaningful layer of privacy and makes it harder for curious strangers to pinpoint our location.

At one point, a relative who works at a school told us their students were talking about watching our channel. That moment really confirmed for us that a little extra anonymity is the right call when it comes to protecting our family life.

Age: The silent statistic

Is your age a badge of honor to be proudly showcased, or will you keep this statistic under wraps, allowing your content to transcend generational boundaries?

Weigh the pros and cons of both approaches and decide what feels right to you. The main pro to revealing your age is that this can create a more authentic persona and enable you to genuinely connect with people in a similar age group. This approach works well for vlog-style personal content.

The main con to revealing your age is that you can become more categorized, judged, and often "put in a box." If you're a proud thirty-year-old, then doing fun back-to-school DIYs for tweens may just seem outright bizarre, even if you're good at it and have the passion. If you plan to create curated, evergreen content that isn't overly personal, then it may be more effective to make your exact age a mystery so as not to typecast yourself into a certain age bracket. This may also make things slightly easier if you'd like to switch up your content genre in the future.

Facing the lens: To be seen or not to be seen

Will your followers glimpse the man behind the curtain? The decision to reveal your face on camera is a cornerstone in creating a connection with your audience. Faceless social media accounts abound nowadays, and we understand why. Putting your face on camera can feel scary and vulnerable. Once you decide to show your face, there is no undo button. That is why many people prefer faceless content, especially in areas like food, travel tips, or DIY projects where the audience mainly cares about what you are doing and not who you are.

The downside to being on camera is that your appearance becomes fair game for criticism. We've been picked apart for everything from acne and makeup to skincare, weight changes, and plenty more. Going through that firsthand has made us completely understand why some creators choose to stay faceless.

We've met creators at YouTube events who never show their face and stick to ASMR or mukbang content. ASMR content refers to relaxing videos that include whispering, tapping, and slow deliberate movements, designed to promote calmness and stress relief in the viewer. Mukbangs are videos where a person eats a large quantity of food, featuring chewing, slurping, and crunching sounds, sometimes filmed from the nose or mouth down. One creator told us she likes filming only from the mouth down while she eats dinner, then jumping right back into caring for her young kids. For her, that separation keeps YouTube and Instagram feeling like a job rather than her entire identity, and she prefers it that way.

There are definite upsides to showing your face, like building a stronger connection with your audience, even though it requires more vulnerability. It makes your brand feel human and helps your audience feel like they know you. People connect with people, not just with pictures of cupcakes or latte art. From a business standpoint, brands are more likely to partner with someone who feels like a personality rather than an anonymous page.

In many cases, showing your face opens the door to more opportunities, like event invites and creator trips. For us, being on camera was a no-brainer since most of our content was "sit-and-talk" style, where you're explaining ideas directly to the viewer. It just made sense. It also let us express our personal style through fashion and makeup. Over the years, we've landed several fashion and beauty campaigns that we undoubtedly wouldn't have if we'd chosen to stay faceless.

Au naturel moments: No makeup, no filters

Are you comfortable showcasing your natural self, makeup-free and straight out of bed? Whether you appear on camera heavily filtered or au naturel really depends on your comfort level as well as what type of content you make. Generally, we favor a made-up look, as it appears more professional on camera, no matter what the content genre is. Even if your content has absolutely nothing to do with makeup, skincare, or appearance, we think it simply looks more professional to wear makeup on camera.

Being more polished on camera has its perks. Wearing makeup can help you look put-together and can even open doors for beauty or product-driven collaborations that fit naturally into your content. The downside is the time it takes to get ready for every shoot.

On the flip side, creators who skip makeup also have their own set of pros and cons. Going barefaced can feel more authentic and confident, but it can also leave you looking a bit more tired or disheveled.

We fall somewhere in the middle. Sometimes we wear makeup, sometimes we don't. It really depends on the situation. For a sponsored sit-down video, we usually aim to look more polished and go for a full makeup look.

At events, it's about a fifty-fifty split. If we're attending a movie premiere where we'll be on a red carpet and photographed by outlets like Getty Images, we definitely put in more effort. Just recently, we dressed up for a premiere where we were professionally photographed and ended up seated near Hollywood actors Seth Green, Macaulay Culkin, and Brenda Song. For moments like that, going the extra mile helps us show up professionally for the PR teams who invite us. But if it's a low-key screening or a nighttime event without real photo ops, we lean more natural and keep our makeup minimal. Over time, we've learned to read the room and decide when it makes sense to dress up or tone it down.

Remember that makeup isn't a tool that only women can use to their advantage! Anyone can wear makeup if they want to. Do you think famous TV personalities like Kelly Ripa, Ryan Seacrest, Oprah Winfrey, Jimmy Kimmel, or Martha Stewart would appear on camera barefaced? Unlikely. You don't need a full glam look, but a little makeup goes a long way in keeping the focus on you instead of any small distractions. Wearing makeup certainly doesn't prove that you're an expert in something; however, it can add a sense of perceived legitimacy.

Makeup can give both men and women alike a creative edge and enhance natural beauty. Creators like Jeffree Star, James Charles, and Patrick Starrr use makeup not only to generate beauty content, but to build up their own successful makeup brands. We even once filmed with a male influencer who dusted on mattifying powder on his shiny bald head so it wouldn't distract viewers. We also have oily skin that tends to look shiny on camera, plus sitting in front of hot lights can make you even more sweaty, so always apply a mattifying powder before filming. We are also happy to use Instagram filters when we feel like it.

We know that putting on makeup each time you film can be tedious and annoying, or maybe it just doesn't feel authentic to who you are. If you'd rather go barefaced and makeup-free, go for it! Some viewers may appreciate the "realness" behind that. There really is no one-size-fits-all answer.

Choosing how much of yourself to show

Will you shoot your videos from the shoulders up or showcase your entire frame? Would you be willing to don a bikini for the world to see? Will you post unedited snapshots? Unveiling your physique is a complex choice.

A lot of this comes down to the kind of content you make and what feels natural to you. If you are doing a sit-and-talk video, then a close-up of your face makes sense. In that situation, a full-body shot would feel unnecessary and distracting.

On the other hand, body positive and fitness creators often build their entire platforms around showing their bodies exactly as they are. They put it all out there, from stretch marks to love handles to changes in weight. For them, that level of openness is the whole point.

Most creators fall somewhere in the middle. For example, we are both fine filming ourselves in swimsuits, but we are not okay with appearing in our underwear. Technically, it shows the same amount of skin, but to us, wearing underwear on camera crosses a personal line. That is just the boundary we have chosen.

If you want to use filters, go ahead. If you choose to edit your photos to slim your waist or tweak your appearance, that's entirely your decision.

There's no "right" or "wrong" here. Just keep in mind that heavy editing can have mixed results. Some viewers can spot warped lines or distorted backgrounds, and overly polished images can unintentionally reinforce unrealistic beauty standards. At the end of the day, what matters most is that you feel comfortable with what you're sharing.

Home sweet home: Privacy versus exposure

How much of your personal space will you share? From your home's geographic location to a complete house tour, each choice shapes the narrative of your digital sanctuary.

This isn't just about aesthetics; it's also about safety. Being too open about where you live can create real risks. A few years ago, "home tour" videos were trending, but they have become less common because people realized they were basically handing out blueprints for potential burglars. In 2021, luxury influencer Tamara Kalinic made headlines when burglars broke into her Paris apartment and stole roughly half a million dollars' worth of designer bags, shoes, and jewelry.

In light of these incidents, many creators decide to keep details about their home and location as limited as possible. Another smart step is to avoid posting your location in real time. For example, share that brunch photo after you've already left the restaurant, not while you're sitting at the table.

Of course, there are exceptions. If your content revolves around your home, such as renovations or home design and decor, then hiding it is not really an option. In that case, it is worth investing in extra security measures, like outdoor cameras or an alarm system. Even asking your neighbors to keep an eye out can make a difference. At the end of the day, staying safe comes first. Your home should always feel like a sanctuary, not a set that leaves you feeling exposed.

Daniel Miller, known as danielxmiller, is a content creator and host who makes vlogs and videos about issues facing the LGBTQ+ community. We asked him about posting in real time, and he said, "I've always been fairly open about my life, as sharing personal experiences has always been at the core of my work. However, one firm boundary I've established is regarding my exact location. Due to safety concerns, I never share my real-time location unless I'm in a very public and secure place. Typically, I don't film anything near my home; I drive at least ten to fifteen minutes away."

Family and unveiling your world

One thing to keep in mind is whether or not you will introduce your family (mom, dad, brother, sister, grandma, grandpa) to your audience, with the intention of offering a more holistic view of your life. Including family and friends is a personal choice, but it isn't just *your* choice. It depends on how they feel about it, too. In our experience, relatives and friends fall into two camps: they either enjoy being part of the show or they absolutely hate it.

Some people enjoy the attention and are happy to pop up as a recurring character. Maybe your grandma chimes in with hilarious commentary on your outfits, your kids do taste tests of your latest recipe, or your best friend drops by every now and then for a quick chat in your vlog. For them, it is all lighthearted fun to guest-star in an episode of your life on the internet. Meanwhile, you get the benefits of fresh and relatable content. It's a win-win!

Then there are those who would rather live a more private life. When we were growing our YouTube channel, we sometimes filmed videos of us pranking our parents. We'd pretend we got tattoos or had a pregnancy scare and film their reactions with hidden cameras. The videos went viral, sometimes even making it onto TV. But our parents were horrified. Our mom, who worked at an elementary school, had her students come up to her and ask if she was "the lady from the Marissa Rachel videos." While we thought it was funny, our parents did not. They eventually banned us from pranking them again.

When you keep information about your family private, you and your family are less likely to be subjected to harassment or ruthless commentary. However, that privacy often prevents you from developing a personal connection with your audience. Audiences often feel more invested in you when they get to know the people (or pets) in your life. That personal connection can be vital to your success. Including friends and family can add a lot of heart and humor to your content, but it only works if everyone is on board.

We grew to learn through our years on social media that even if something makes for good content, it's not always worth the personal repercussions you may face. It's important to get consent from your friends and family and respect the privacy of those who don't wish to appear in online content.

Love and loss: Romantic relationships on display

Navigating the delicate balance between sharing and shielding romantic relationships can often be the key to inner peace and avoiding public scrutiny.

Oftentimes, when a couple makes their relationship public on social media and builds a strong personal brand with their significant other, they feel indebted to their audience that "shipped" the relationship. If the couple decides to break up, they feel like they need to cry on camera or overshare details about why the relationship ended. But, in our opinion, you don't owe your audience anything of the sort.

Creators often forget this. If it makes you feel better to type out a cryptic Instagram story, saying something like "I'm going through a rough time, thank you all for the support and for respecting my privacy," or even go radio silent, that's totally acceptable! The only person you owe and have a responsibility to is yourself.

For example, Shanna has strict boundaries when it comes to showcasing her romantic life. "My husband has very little social media presence. Aside from a Facebook page from his college days, the only social media platform on which he is interested in being active is LinkedIn. I have gone to great lengths to exclude him from my social media while still showcasing my own life. Even when I posted my wedding on social media, I was very careful only to use shots of myself wearing my wedding dress. This might seem excessive to some people, but it is my boundary. That's what I feel comfortable with, and I have never once questioned this decision."

Most creators set personal boundaries when it comes to deciding how much to share about their romantic lives. Amber Scholl, a shopping content creator, says, "I'm a pretty open book. There's not much I don't share . . . though I do love a cheeky secret that keeps people guessing. My love life is public domain, but only the highlight reel. For every story I tell, there are ten I don't."

Emotional transparency: Posting the peaks and valleys

As a creator, it's important to consider whether you want to share only a highlight reel of your life or candidly share moments of vulnerability, including the bad days. Pro tip: while it's certainly commendable to "keep it real" and post honest, authentic content, you also need to consider what's best for your mental health. For some people, it can feel therapeutic to film themselves crying and talking things out. But that's not the case for everyone. We personally feel far worse when we post ourselves expressing our innermost feelings to a large audience that may or may not be understanding. When we are dealing with hard times, we prefer to confide in a few close friends rather than our entire audience.

Social media influencer Melissa Tierney says, "I'm someone who likes to keep my personal life pretty private. So yes, I shared content about my wedding, but I'm not going to share the stressful parts of planning it. I feel like my brand is more happy and joyful. Getting online and crying or complaining just isn't me. As a creator, you get to decide how open and vulnerable you want to be."

We, too, usually try to create a happier, lighter space on our channel. Being too open and vulnerable online can be exhausting. It can leave you with what feels like an emotional hangover after you share too much. If you decide to share your vulnerable moments or the bad times in your life, you also need to be prepared to deal with criticism. People on the internet can be quick to judge or use your honesty against you. Unfortunately, this does not only come from random trolls. Sometimes it comes from people you actually know.

Our best advice is to move carefully and check in with yourself often. After you post something vulnerable, do you feel lighter, freer, and eager to seek connection with your community, or do you feel an immediate urge to take it down? If something ever feels off, trust that feeling. You can always delete, adjust, or change direction. Your peace of mind matters more than a post.

The stuff you don't discuss at dinner: Politics, religion, and money

To post or not to post about controversial topics like politics, religion, and money? The decision to share your beliefs can cement your stance in the digital realm, but it can also invite criticism, arguments, and serious consequences.

For example, are you comfortable sharing your income, spending habits, or financial details? It can be a tough balance between being transparent and keeping some privacy. Remember when it became trendy to post "what I spend in a day" videos? Some of them were honest and relatable, while others came across as bragging or showing off.

Politics can be even more complicated. The internet can feel like a minefield during heated times. Every major political event seems to lead to someone getting canceled or even fired over a single emotional post. Before you share, ask yourself: Could this hurt my career? Could this offend or upset people? Does this reflect who I am and what I stand for? Is it worth it?

Some creators feel pressured to speak up about every single issue or current event that happens in the world. Constantly posting about every issue often turns into performative activism. It's completely acceptable to remain silent.

There will always be people complaining that you aren't posting about this subject or that event, but we are not reporters for CNN or experts on every topic. For example, during the pandemic, keyboard warriors (also known as haters) would often prey on creators who were still posting about fashion, beauty, and other topics deemed more trivial. But a creator who's knowledgeable about makeup might not also be an expert in public health, so it wouldn't make any sense for them to change lanes and post about that topic. If viewers are more interested in watching scientific content, there are plenty of other accounts to follow instead.

Whenever there is a current event or issue that everyone feels the need to post about, remind yourself that you can always choose to stay in your lane. What matters most is what you do in your real life, not what you post online.

Content creation: Scripted versus unscripted

Will your content follow a carefully scripted and curated narrative, presenting a polished image to your audience, or will you embrace an unscripted, vlog-style approach that offers a raw glimpse into your daily experiences?

We'll let you in on a secret: you don't need to pick just one. You can always switch between more sentimental/personal vlogs and scripted comedy skits. Scripted content can help you look professional and creative, while unscripted moments make you seem more personable. A good mix keeps your content dynamic. Both approaches are obviously beneficial for growth and fostering a connection with the viewers.

Edgy elements: Cursing, inebriation, and substance use

Where do you draw the line on edgy content? From profanity and alcohol to the complexities of substance use, each choice shapes your digital persona. For some creators, cursing and swearing is about "keeping it real." It's part of their voice and how they naturally talk. There is no denying that edgy content is effective at grabbing attention. It can be funny, shocking, and relatable in a way that polished, picture-perfect posts are not. People will find you to be more relatable if you reveal flaws and imperfections, which can expand your reach to people who resonate with your candid spirit.

However, some creators avoid this kind of content because they fear the real-life consequences of their grandparents, professors, or employers seeing an unprofessional or inappropriate side of them. Edgy elements can limit your audience to a certain demographic, usually older teens or adults who also swear, use alcohol, and so on. Being edgy comes with other risks. You might attract hate comments or even entire forums dedicated to criticizing you. Things you say can easily be taken out of context and turned into something they were never meant to be. The internet loves an easy villain, and not everyone will care about the nuance of your words or intentions.

Even if you are comfortable with that, remember that some brands may not be. Many prefer to stay away from creators who could be seen as controversial. You might find that your options for brand collaborations are more limited if your content leans too far into the edgy side.

To determine what's best for you and your content, ask yourself some questions about your long-term goals. Are you looking for more curated opportunities from brands? Do you want to make yourself into a brand and personality? If you don't intend on making content creation a full-time gig, then maybe you are fine with being more candid. However, as we mentioned earlier, don't forget that there could be consequences to people in your everyday life seeing your "risqué" content.

A Journey of Self-Discovery

These decisions are complex, requiring thoughtful consideration. Maybe some of these choices are easy for you to make, but others require more reflection. It's also important to remember that these boundaries will almost certainly evolve. You may start out showcasing everything about your life and slowly change that decision as time goes on. On the flip side, you might start out more private and guarded, then gradually become more relaxed in front of your audience.

For example, it's often the case that when people first start out posting themselves online, they're fixated on appearance and presentation. They spend ages fussing over the angles and the lighting, trying to look as optimally attractive as possible. Over time, that need to make everything perfect usually starts to fade. You get more comfortable with the little slip-ups and imperfect moments. Eventually, you stop stressing about editing out every tiny mistake and start leaning into being real instead.

Perfection is often the enemy of success. Spending three hours every time you want to take a selfie isn't a practical use of time. Doing fifty-three takes of every video is unsustainable. The more you can let go of the idea of "content perfection," the more productive you'll be. After all, you're a content creator team of one; you do not have limitless resources the way a big-budget Marvel movie being made in Hollywood might. Working smart is a virtue. Perfection is not expected.

Our advice is to begin with a guarded approach, gradually unveiling layers of your life as you become more at ease with your digital self. Like adding spice to a recipe, it's easy to add in more flavors; it's much harder to take them out.

Setting your boundaries is not just a strategy; it's an ongoing journey of self-discovery.

8

Kids on Social Media

A few years ago, we were asked to speak at a Career Day at a local middle school. Armed with a presentation about the world of social media influencing, we aimed to engage classrooms of seventh graders with anecdotes from our journey, highlighting positive messages about hard work, goal-setting, and using online influence to give back to your community. However, when Career Day arrived, a wave of nervousness washed over us when we learned we were scheduled to present right after a structural engineer. Being a structural engineer is considered a "real job." Would our careers seem as legitimate, interesting, or worthy of respect?

Fortunately for us, the students were not only receptive but genuinely excited to hear about our experience as social media influencers. They loved seeing pictures from our collaborations with renowned influencers, featuring familiar faces like JoJo Siwa, Maddie Ziegler, and Chloé Lukasiak from *Dance Moms*.

While answering questions about how to get more Instagram followers and whether we had ever met [insert tween TikTok or YouTube star here], we started to consider the dangers of teens and youth using the internet. We're not referring to the obvious dangers of online predators, but rather the subtle threats of low self-esteem, depression, comparison to others, and screen time addiction.

While our experience at Career Day was rewarding, it left us pondering an unsettling question that we know the structural engineer did not face: Are we unintentionally glamorizing online stardom to impressionable kids?

When kids use the internet, and especially when they have a social media presence, they need to be protected. And not just from creeps and bullies, but from the pressure, the performative culture, and the digital chaos that even adults struggle with. Honestly, if the internet is confusing for us, imagine trying to navigate it with a third-grade education and a developing frontal lobe.

In this chapter, we provide an overview of the various concerns related to kids and social media, outlining the pros and cons of different approaches for mitigating these concerns. We also share our thoughts as influencers with lots of social media experience as well as Shanna's perspective as a parent.

The Great Debate

There are so many layers to the whole "kids on social media" conversation. We didn't fully realize how complicated it was until Shanna was about to become a mom herself. Somewhere between reading reviews on bottle sterilizers and watching videos on how to swaddle a baby, we started wondering about what happens when kids grow up online.

Depending on who you ask, the topic can get pretty heated. It's not just a straightforward question; it's more like a tangled ball of opinions, ethics, emotions, and baby pictures. Some people treat it like a parenting hill to die on, never posting a single photo of their kid's face. Others shrug and say, "It's fine," while posting every milestone.

The consensus among parents is a shared commitment to safeguarding children online. Considering the permanence of a social media footprint, influencers and parents alike face a critical decision. Will their digital legacy showcase moments of joy or inadvertently expose private and potentially embarrassing moments? The narrative surrounding children on the internet calls for a delicate and thoughtful approach.

At the heart of this nuanced debate, there are really two different scenarios:

> **Parents posting *about* their kids on their own accounts.** This is when parents post birth announcements, baby photos, Halloween costumes, and first-day-of-school pics. In this scenario, the grown-ups are running the show. The parent is in control of the content, the account, and the audience.
>
> **Kids eventually using their *own* social media accounts.** This is when kids view, engage with, and create content online all on their own.

When Kids Are Featured on Their Parents' Accounts

When parents share content about their children on their own pages, it tends to be more "controlled." Parents decide what's posted, who sees it, and how much of their child's life is being shared. On the surface, this seems pretty harmless, especially when these parents are just posting cute moments on a private account so that Grandma can watch the kids grow. Still, that doesn't mean it's without debate.

There are three ways parents typically feature kids online.

Some parents decide to feature their kids' faces in a limited sense. These parents will post the pictures on private accounts that are only accessible to friends and family, allowing them to share their children's growth more easily with friends and family members who live far away.

Other parents take a hardline approach that their kids' faces will never appear on social media. Their goal is to protect their child's privacy and instill safety at all times. Parents might choose to post only the back of their child's head or cover their child's face with a strategically placed emoji.

Some parents opt for a different path, incorporating their kids into content that features only the positive moments, like photos of their children smiling or laughing rather than negative or embarrassing content, like a video of a tantrum. A notable ethical stance emerges among those who integrate their children into content: a commitment to not exploit vulnerable moments. This conscious choice reflects a desire to preserve a positive legacy for their children's digital footprint.

There are vastly different opinions when it comes to featuring children online. Some argue that a child isn't equipped to make such a complex decision about appearing in digital content, while others have no qualms about openly sharing their kids with the world.

That said, a lot of parents do change their approach as their kids get older. Parents might post adorable photos of their toddler with wild hair and spaghetti all over their face, but as that kid gets older, those parents' posts start to change. Why? Because once kids start school and interact with the outside world (teachers, classmates, other parents), things get more real. Suddenly, there's this awareness that someone might form an opinion about your kid before even meeting them. And that doesn't sit right for a lot of us.

Another concern is that once your kid starts outgrowing babyhood and growing into their face, they become recognizable. And that opens up a whole new can of worms. There's something a little unsettling about a stranger walking up to your kid in Target saying, "Hi, Ella! I've seen your birthday party pictures!" That kind of interaction might come from a good place, but it can still be scary for the kid, not to mention unsafe. In our opinion, the "right way" to post about kids isn't really about waiting for some magical age when they can genuinely approve of their parents' content. It's about constantly reevaluating what feels right, what feels safe, and how to balance connection with protection. After all, parenting is basically a nonstop series of decisions we make for our kids, hopefully with love, thoughtfulness, and a little common sense.

Thinking beyond just photos

One crucial thing to remember when we're talking about kids' social media presence and digital footprint: it's not just about photos. Most of the conversations around this topic focus only on images. Should you post your child's face? Should you blur it out? Use emojis? But there's a whole other side to privacy that doesn't get talked about enough: what you're sharing in words.

During our research, one of the most surprising, and eye-opening, things we came across was about protecting your child's name (like their full, legal name) online.

So many of us have seen heartfelt birth announcements in our feeds. They usually include the baby's full name, date of birth, time of birth, weight, length, and so on. It's practically a blueprint for identity theft. And parents don't share this info because they're careless. They share it because they're proud! They love their kids, they're excited, and they want to share that joy with the people in their lives. But oversharing, even unintentionally, can create risks we don't always consider in the moment.

If you're concerned about the safety of your child, consider that some parents are choosing to go a different route. There are some alternatives that can allow more anonymity when featuring your kids in your posts.

For example, instead of sharing your child's legal name, you can use a nickname or even a totally made-up name that's something unrelated to their real identity. That way, if someone googles your child one day, they're not greeted with an archive of personal milestones and baby stats. You can choose to skip the last name altogether or use just an initial. Some refer to their kids by cute code names like "Little Bean" or "Mr. N."

It's not about being paranoid. It's about being intentional. Because once something's online, it can stick around forever. Kids deserve the chance to define their digital footprint on their terms, not just ours. So when you're thinking about what you post, sure, consider the photos. But also take a second look at what you're saying. Sometimes, the details we don't think twice about are the ones that matter most.

Making money with kid-fluencing

The biggest criticisms seem to be reserved for the family vloggers, those who make a living off of posting their children's every move.

Even though social media might feel casual, once money enters the picture, it's business. And when your kids are part of that business, whether through brand deals, ads, or affiliate links, they deserve the same care and consideration as any other professional.

Traditional child labor laws exist for kid actors and models who appear in commercials, movies, and TV shows. Those laws help make sure they're protected, fairly compensated, and not overworked. Until very recently, though, there were no equivalent laws for kids appearing in online content, even if that content brought in serious income. That's slowly starting to change, with some states introducing legislation to protect young digital creators and ensure they're compensated fairly. But we're still in the early stages.

Illinois became the first US state to pass a law specifically protecting child influencers. The legislation, which took effect on July 1, 2024, mandates that children under age sixteen who appear in at least 30 percent of a parent or guardian's monetized online content over a thirty-day period must be compensated. Parents are required to set aside a portion of the earnings in a trust account for the child to access upon turning eighteen. If parents fail to comply, the child has the right to take legal action.

Following Illinois's lead, other states, including Minnesota, Utah, and California, have begun considering similar legislation to safeguard the rights and earnings of child influencers.

So if you're thinking about including your kids in monetized content, it's worth taking a hard look at where the money's going, what boundaries you're setting, and how you're protecting your child, both emotionally and financially.

Whether legally required to or not, you can't go wrong setting aside a portion of the money the content earns for your child. When you put it into an account for your child to access when they're older, it's a way of saying, "Hey, you helped build this, so you should benefit from it, too." Some parents argue that they create content that features their kids so that they can build a financial cushion for their child's future. Making money from content that features your kids brings up some pretty big ethical concerns as well. One of the most important things is to never force a child to perform. The best family creators make sure their kids are having fun, never forced to film, and allowed to opt out when they're not in the mood. Because at the end of the day, they're kids first, not content.

When Kids Have Their Own Social Media Accounts

There is no shortage of dangers kids are exposed to when they have their own social media accounts. Two of the most significant risks are online predators and crippling self-esteem issues.

Online predators

When it comes to online predators, we heard a story during our research that really stuck with us. Honestly, it still gives us chills.

We read about an intelligent, kind, twenty-two-year-old Stanford student who seemed like the kind of kid you'd assume had every advantage. His parents were both doctors, and he grew up in a supportive, loving home. The type of environment where you'd think surely someone like him wouldn't fall victim to an online predator. His parents gave him all the standard lectures, set all the right boundaries, and warned him not to talk to strangers online.

But still . . . he did. And what happened next was something no parent ever wants to imagine. When he was just thirteen years old, he met someone online who he believed was a thirteen-year-old girl. The girl flirted with him, sent him nude photos of herself, and eventually asked him to send nude photos of himself. Once he sent the photos, the person he had been talking to revealed that they were not a thirteen-year-old girl but, in fact, an adult man. The man then pressured him to send more explicit photos, as well as videos, and threatened to blackmail the boy if he didn't by sending the explicit content to all of the boy's classmates. The boy finally told his parents, who contacted the police. He stopped communicating with the man and learned a difficult but important lesson. Not everyone is who they appear to be, and sending sensitive information—or in this case, compromising photos—can be extremely dangerous.

It doesn't matter how bright your kids are and how much you lecture them on the dangers of online predators; kids are still naïve and can be manipulated by people with bad intentions. If you're going to let your kid dive into the internet, at the very least, make sure their devices have safety features in place.

Self-esteem issues

While online predators are the most obvious risk of kids having their own social media accounts, there's another danger that is far less visible to spot but way more common. Consuming social media can erode self-esteem.

Even adults have experienced this. It's that creeping sense of inadequacy after scrolling through someone else's perfect vacation photos and glowing highlight reels. It's that weight of regret you feel when you view the profiles of people who seem to have their entire life together while you're still lounging in pajamas. If social media can make adults feel like they're not good enough, imagine what it can do to kids who are still figuring out who they are.

When we were growing up, our comparison pool was limited to the number of kids in our school. Now? Kids can compare themselves to everyone. The entire internet is a stage, and everyone else looks like they're winning. Whether it's trends like posting your college acceptance letters or showing off meticulous teen glow-ups, it's a nonstop feed of brutal comparison. It's not just celebrity photoshoots that make a teenager feel insecure. It's seeing highlight reels from their peers—their classmates and teammates—that hits the hardest. Seeing someone you actually know living their "best life" can sting way more than watching a pop star on a yacht.

The Benefits of Social Media

Despite the potential risks, social media isn't all bad for kids. Here, we'll get into some of the benefits of kids diving into the online world and what those experiences can lead to.

A lifeline

Online communities can offer a sense of belonging, confidence, and identity, especially when they might not be getting that in real life. If a kid feels isolated or different at school, the internet can connect them to like-minded people who understand them. It can help them find their people, their passions, and their voice. Before the internet, if you didn't fit in at school, then you just dealt with being an outcast. Now, a kid who doesn't fit in with the other kids at their school can find entire communities that say, "Hey, you're not weird! You're awesome." And that kind of validation can be powerful.

So yes, social media can chip away at self-worth. But it can also build it. The key is to help kids use social media in a productive way that supports their growth.

A creative outlet

One thing that frequently gets overlooked in the whole "Is social media bad for kids?" debate is that there is a world of difference between consuming social media and creating content.

Scrolling endlessly can be mindless and a waste of time. But creating content? That's a different story. It can be incredibly creative, intentional, and even educational. Coming up with an idea, planning a story, picking a concept, and building out a strategy requires real work. And when kids get into it, they can tap into a whole range of skills. They might design costumes for skits, experiment with recipes, learn to use camera angles, edit videos, or play with lighting. They might even dive into stop-motion animation or Claymation, write and share their own music, or post their artwork. That's technical skills, creative muscles, and digital literacy all rolled into one!

One high school teacher we spoke to pointed out that most teens aren't creating original content. Most of them are just scrolling or reposting memes. And when they do create a post, they are often just resharing something they saw and not sharing any creative work. So while the potential is there, most kids aren't tapping into it yet.

That's why it's important to reframe the conversation. Kids using social media isn't necessarily a bad thing or a good thing. It's all about how they use it. Are they mindlessly consuming, or are they actively creating? Are they learning skills and expressing themselves, or just chasing likes and reposting trends?

Social media can be a powerful tool for creativity and connection, but it requires guidance, boundaries, and, let's be honest, a little adult supervision to make sure it's used in a safe, positive, and productive way.

9

Handling Hate Comments

Hate comments can elicit some of the most confusing, contradictory, and ambivalent feelings ever! Some creators decide to view hate comments as a form of flattery, rationalizing that if people really don't like what you have to say, then your content must be reaching a vast audience.

Zoe Unlimited, a lifestyle and marketing creator, says, "Anything worth doing is going to get hate. Haters are just confused fans. They're spending so much time on you, paying attention to your every move, directing traffic to you. It's free marketing. Haters stay focused on winners. Winners stay focused on winning."

However, receiving hate comments can also be an extraordinary hit to your ego. These haters may be people you know or complete strangers. Either way, it stings when people carelessly disparage your entire livelihood. Enough hate comments can even lead to a creator being "canceled." So what can you do about it? Which actions do you take, if any? Do you reply? Confront the hater? Make content about the hate comment? Delete the comment? The not-so-simple answer is that it will depend on each situation.

That being said, how you manage hate comments remains a controversial topic with many pros and cons to consider, which we help you weigh in this chapter. But before you decide what action to take in the face of hate comments, it's important to assess how that comment (and your reaction) will impact you and your brand.

The Impact of Hate Comments

Most PR people in charge of hiring influencers are not meticulously combing through every comment. Most brands won't notice some scattered hate comments, unless you're involved in a national scandal or getting "canceled" on a larger, more public level. After all, brands can come under extreme heat by sponsoring or affiliating with creators who get too much negative attention. We once heard a PR representative say that they stopped inviting Jake Paul and Logan Paul to their events because of Jake Paul's drug addiction debacle and Logan Paul's "walking through a suicide forest" video, which famously featured a blurred-out face of a deceased individual. The truth is, more often than not, hate comments will not heavily affect your brand or business. It will depend on the scale and level of comments you receive. For example, if 20 percent of the comments you receive are negative and 80 percent are positive, then you likely don't have anything to worry about.

So if a small percentage of hate comments don't really affect your money or opportunities too much, then what does it affect?

It can drastically affect your mental state and well-being *if* you let it. If you post your content without unshakable inner confidence, you can easily be upset by mean comments. Several years ago, while on a brand trip, we got to our hotel room and immediately checked the comment section of the latest video we had posted. (This was back during our "We need to see what people are saying about us and desperately micromanage comments" phase.) Lots of hate comments stood out to us. One even called Marissa "Marissa Ratchet," which made us belly laugh because we appreciated the play on words. For a split second, we felt alarmed at the sheer level of hate comments we'd been receiving. After all, the video had several hundred thousand views and was gaining more and more every hour. But then we looked up, and we remembered where we were . . . on a brand trip to Boston, flown out by 20th Century Studios to visit the set of a new X-Men movie and create promotional content. We'd been booked in the nicest private suite at the best hotel in the city, according to the driver who picked us up from the airport. It was then that it occurred to us that all the people that made this trip possible—the managers, movie network people, and PR representatives—didn't care that we had a substantial number of hate comments on our recent video. We had earned an incredible opportunity, and our brand was thriving.

So next time you start to panic about hate comments, consider the bigger picture. Is your content still doing well, despite a few haters? The only time you should be truly worried about hate comments is when they're severely affecting your brand, earnings, or mental health in a detrimental way.

When Hate Comments Become a Problem

We've all heard "Sticks and stones will break my bones, but names will never hurt me." We *know* we shouldn't let others dictate how we feel about ourselves. We know we have the power to maintain control over emotions, and that we shouldn't be too reactive to the words of those around us.

However, what if your career was at stake? What if too many hate comments ultimately impacted the overall perception of your brand and cost you opportunities?

So, we've discussed that hate comments aren't always a big issue; now let's shift to talking about when they do become an issue, as well as navigating the intricacies of what to do when you find yourself overwhelmed with comments that don't align with your brand.

Consider the negatives of the hate comments on your social media. Maybe they've affected your motivation and mental health. Or maybe you're worried a family member, friend, partner, coworker, or boss will see it and think something negative about you. Sometimes the algorithm unfortunately reaches those you hoped it wouldn't reach.

Whatever the pros and cons are, you need to weigh out the experience as a whole. What side has more weight on it, the positive or the negative side? The only time to worry is when the negative side overwhelms the positive side.

Some days things will feel overwhelmingly negative. Imagine you've just had two brand deals fall through, didn't get invited to the event that you really wanted to go to, and saw the Instagram stories and posts of everyone else who did go. On top of that, you received thirty-six hate comments on your new Instagram reel insulting your appearance. Seems pretty hopeless, right? But it's important to remember that social media is a rollercoaster ride; there are highs and lows. You enjoy the highs to the fullest and ride out the lows. Sometimes a low could feel like it's lasting weeks, months, or even years. Especially with haters and hate comments. But it's vital to remember that haters only have the power you give to them.

How to Address Hate Comments

So what the heck are you supposed to do when you get a negative comment? Many different people will have many different answers to this question. The boring cookie-cutter response is always going to be "it depends." First, you need to determine what you want your response to achieve. Are you trying to inform them of something in a genuine and neutral way? Or are you responding purely out of ego, where your energy is vengeful and spiteful? If you decide to react to the hate comment, you have a few options to consider.

Responding positively

Believe it or not, this was one of the first ways we handled hate comments back in 2012 when we first received them. Marissa had been just coming out of her shell and appearing in front of the camera with sit-and-talk content. The overwhelming majority of hate comments were usually about her voice. It was always some variation of "Her voice is sooooooo annoying" or "Omg, I cannot stand her voice!" For a time, she'd respond with "Thanks so much for commenting :) Hope you have a great day!" The beauty of this was that it often confused the commenter. Some would even retract their statements and say, "Wow, you're so kind," obviously very puzzled by the response.

Sometimes we'd see that haters were also content creators, so we would comment something positive about their videos. One hate-comment writer had posted a cover of Maroon 5's "Payphone," and we responded to her hate comment by telling her she had a beautiful voice. She was very taken aback by our compliment.

Doing this definitely requires you to be the bigger person, which can be difficult. However, it's important that your positive response doesn't have a passive-aggressive tone. The point is to not stoop to the commenter's level. By showing kindness and maturity, you let the naysayers know that their comments don't affect you on a deeper level.

Responding negatively

Fighting back seems to be much more of a common response for creators who feel justified when someone is attacking their looks, personality, family, livelihood, or any aspect of content that they posted. For example, we've seen a man comment on a woman's post, calling her an "Ugly 4/10," with the female creator responding with "Wow, hope you don't talk to your girlfriend that way. I sure do feel bad for her." This makes it abundantly clear to the commenter and everyone else reading the response that the creator has reviewed the hater's account. To some creators, responding with something sassy can definitely make it seem like you've "won the argument" and can feel empowering. Just keep in mind that some people might think that you're being petty by responding like this.

Not responding and leaving the hate comment up

You know what internet trolls can't stand? Posting a hate comment (maybe even through an anonymous account) and having absolutely no one comment on or react to it. Trolls live for using social media to gain attention, clout, or traction by amplifying negativity. Some creators prefer to leave all comments up, regardless of whether they are positive or negative, because "engagement is engagement."

There are other reasons to leave up an unfavorable comment. For example, we posted content about a unique dining experience where you watch a movie and are served fine dining dishes that match what's happening on screen. Some people commented, saying it looked cool but felt too expensive. We left those comments up. They weren't glowing reviews, but they were honest. We're more likely to leave up unfavorable comments that still come across as respectful. People are allowed to have legitimate complaints, and if they express them in a thoughtful way, we don't mind as much.

Not responding and deleting the comments or blocking the commenter

Sometimes the most powerful response is no response at all, whether that's not replying or simply just deleting comments that you feel don't belong on your content. This is how we prefer to handle hate comments. If we get a comment that's outright mean, perverted, derogatory, or just plain untrue, we delete it and, depending on the context, may even block the person or restrict them from our accounts (meaning that we and they are the only ones who can view their comments).

Why do we do this? Yes, to keep the haters at bay. But also to control our overall brand and maintain our image. If the comment is posted under a sponsored or collaborative post, there is a good chance we'll delete it to maintain integrity and rapport. Since our brand is more curated and features a lot of branded content, this approach makes sense for us.

However, if your content is more personality-focused or vlog-style, maybe it's worth leaving up the negative comments for engagement. Again, it's up to you, and your approach should reflect your social media goals.

Remember when we mentioned leaving up some critiques about a fine dining experience? Well, a different individual left a comment completely trashing the whole thing. She said the food was cold, the experience was terrible, and we only liked it because we're influencers. We chose to delete that one. This was a collaboration with the brand, and her comment came off as rude and inaccurate.

We've definitely had those moments when we imagine writing out a snarky little comment along the lines of "If you'd like to enjoy complimentary experiences like this, feel free to become a creator and start asking for event invites!" smirking to ourselves. And then we just delete the hate comment. Poof. Gone. Like it never happened.

Why did we let it go? Because we envision the brand looking at their latest collaboration post with us and seeing our petty remarks. We feel potential embarrassment just thinking about how unprofessional it would make us appear. The truth is, the hate comment was disparaging both the brand and ourselves as creators.

Another course of action is turning off comments altogether. Feeling in control of your social media is important, and that includes the comments section. Jessica Rae, who goes by the username @omg_Jess on TikTok and discusses lifestyle and pop culture, says, "I had a TikTok go viral and the comment section started resorting to personal attacks calling me ugly. So I decided to remove the ability to leave comments on that video. The beautiful thing about when you create your own content is that you can choose the energy that comes at you."

The important thing to remember is that this is *your* platform that *you* built. You don't need to allow people to have the power and control that they so desperately crave by leaving attention-seeking comments. Is there a comment that's keeping you up at night? Block and repeat! Our mentality is this: if someone truly feels like they need to say something about us and that we're clouding their freedom of speech, then they're free to go create their own content about it and upload it on their own channel. Reaction videos certainly can gain views and attention, but having a hater watch their comment fade into oblivion and get blocked from leaving future comments can be a very humbling experience for them. Remember to take ownership of your comment section, because, after all, it's your brand and you have the final say on what stays and what goes.

Making a video response about the hater

Some creators choose to respond to hate comments by creating a video in which they call out the haters. We've seen videos in which women who have received hate comments about their appearance give the commenters a taste of their own medicine. In the response videos, the women display screenshots of the rude and degrading comments men leave on screen, and immediately after that, they show a photo of the man who left the comment. The implication is that it's comedic and ironic that an unattractive man would critique a beautiful woman's appearance. These videos always seem to get a lot of views and engagement, being flooded with likes and comments.

This strategy might work for you if you get a large number of these comments and you'd like to respond to multiple comments at once and capitalize on hate comments for content. If that kind of content aligns with your brand and makes you feel good, then go for it. These types of videos also are more likely to go viral for their comical and light vibe. The downside is that you are giving the haters attention.

It's important to ask yourself *why* you are responding. We actually did respond to a few of the comments that complained about the cost of the fine dining movie experience we attended. Our replies explained that the event organizers email out coupon codes every month and give away five free tickets for each showing. This felt like a productive response that benefited ourselves, the brand, and the person leaving the comment.

Some Will Love You, Some Will Hate You

Creator Daniel Miller says, "Something I wish I'd known earlier is that you can't please everyone. Some viewers will love you; others won't—and that's okay. Negative comments can be hurtful, but they're inevitable if you're putting yourself out there for the world to see. Even today, mean comments still affect me. There have been times I had to delete videos because the negativity was too overwhelming, and I was just the interviewer. Knowing this early on [in your social media career] can help prepare you for when it inevitably happens, although it's important to know that no matter how much you prepare, the emotion still seeps through."

It's important to remember that all influencers who have posted enough videos receive hate at some point. Whether you're an influencer with millions of followers or you have a modest personal account, the internet is filled with hate. It's best to expect it without worrying too much. Don't let the prospect of negativity keep you from creating. Prep yourself for the hate, but recognize that it's typically short-lived.

10

Confronting Cancel Culture

Imagine this: you've built up a social media empire over the last few years, uploaded hundreds of videos, and created an engaged following. Maybe you hit 100,000 followers or even 1,000,000 followers, and things are going really well. You're getting opportunities left and right and being paid thousands of dollars for branded content. Every day, you get deliveries filled with free PR samples that ordinarily people would be paying hundreds of dollars for. Everything is going incredibly well.

Then suddenly, your content begins to go viral. It's reposted thousands of times and flooded with comments. But there's a catch: none of the comments are good. They're all extremely negative, and clearly, viewers do not agree with the content of your post. The hate doesn't just make up 10 percent of the comments, or even 20 percent, but a staggering 95 percent of the comments are critical. Your brand sponsors begin pulling out, and your opportunities begin to get canceled one by one. But it's not just the opportunities; it's bigger than that. *You've* been canceled.

In this chapter, we support you through the rough waters of being a social media influencer when online criticism goes beyond just a few hate comments and affects your brand and business on a much larger scale. We include examples of what to do in this scenario and how to navigate the drama, do damage control, and avoid getting yourself into this situation in the first place.

The good news is, most of the time, influencers can come back from being canceled. Even seemingly damaged brands and creators are salvageable. However, you have to respond appropriately. There are people who unintentionally dig themselves into a giant hole, and only the people who know what to do are capable of digging themselves out. We're here to provide you with that guidance. Though we hope you never need it!

What Is Cancel Culture?

Cancel culture is a relatively easy concept to understand. Basically, it's the withdrawal of public support, often on social media platforms, as a result of a person's offensive actions or opinions. When you think of the term "canceled," several influencers, political figures, celebrities, and people might spring to mind. Everyone knows of someone who's been canceled.

There are many different reasons for getting canceled. You can have an unpopular opinion or viewpoint, do something that people disagree with, share too much, share too little, rub people the wrong way, or do a multitude of other things that may be perceived as undesirable or unacceptable.

A Cancel Culture Case Study

So what happens when a creator unintentionally sinks their own battleship? Let's look at YouTuber Nikki Phillippi, a lifestyle content creator who has been in this space for well over a decade and has posted more than a thousand videos on YouTube. Nikki frequently posted vlogs about daily life, routines, skincare, beauty, food, and more. She often booked sponsored campaigns for a variety of different beauty/fashion/home brands, and in recent years she became a mom vlogger. In 2021, Nikki and her husband Dan filmed a video titled "We have some really sad news." In the extremely detailed, twenty-four-minute video, they discuss their decision to put down their beloved nine-year-old dog named Bowser. They go into detail about how Bowser was getting aggressive and attacking their young son, but also gave additional context about how they let their son disrupt Bowser while he was eating.

At one point in the video, Nikki Phillippi's husband made an offhand comment about Bowser that many viewers found disturbing. He said, "In the moment, I'm thinking, I grew up with the movie *Old Yeller*, and I wanted to pick Bowser up by the back of the neck and take him into the backyard and put him down right there." The reference, drawn from a well-known movie in which a boy is forced to shoot his rabid dog, was met with immediate backlash. Within hours, hundreds of videos criticizing the Phillippis began surfacing online.

Viewers questioned many aspects of the couple's twenty-four-minute explanation, including why they chose to do a photoshoot with the dog near their child shortly before having him euthanized. They also challenged the reasons the couple gave for not rehoming Bowser. Nikki and Dan claimed they would still be legally responsible if he ever harmed someone in the future, but many felt this excuse didn't hold up. Commenters pointed out that Bowser was healthy and could have easily been rehomed with a child-free family or placed in a qualified facility.

Others took issue with the idea that the timing of his death was convenient because the Phillippis were about to move, and Bowser didn't handle change well. These details were picked apart in reaction videos, social media posts, and even traditional news coverage. The overwhelming response was negative, with most viewers expressing outrage and demanding justice for the bull terrier.

In other words, all the details Nikki and Dan gave about the situation did not serve them well whatsoever. Think of a courtroom or an officer reading you the Miranda rights—"Anything you say can and will be used against you in a court of law." The same is typically true for social media. You don't owe anyone all the details of your life, but when you choose to share, it can backfire drastically. Many accused the couple of capitalizing on the tragedy of their euthanized dog for views. Some angry viewers even went so far as to publicly message sponsors demanding that they drop the Phillippis as partners and never work with them again.

Following the controversy, Nikki announced a break from social media, citing death threats. She turned off comments on all platforms to protect her mental health.

In her return video two months later, she revealed that cancel culture had cost them most of their brand deals and income for the year. She stated that she felt they had initially downplayed the severity of Bowser's behavior and that the backlash had been severe. To re-engage with her audience, Nikki launched her Patreon, inviting only subscribers to comment. Her YouTube and Instagram comments remained restricted. Upon her return, Nikki framed the experience as a learning opportunity, emphasizing personal growth and resilience despite the trauma of being "canceled."

So, what could they have done differently?

For starters, making a YouTube video about something so controversial is a huge risk. Even when a dog is put down for health reasons, people tend to have strong and mixed reactions. Choosing to put down a healthy dog is even more emotionally charged. It's not surprising that kind of content would be met with intense backlash. If they truly felt the need to acknowledge Bowser's passing, a simple Instagram story with minimal text would have been enough. Most viewers likely wouldn't have pressed for details. But the way Nikki and Dan presented the news gave some viewers the impression that the real goal was to exploit a tragedy for attention and ad revenue.

What Can You Do to Mitigate Getting Canceled

Let's go over some key takeaways so that you can avoid getting canceled. There are plenty of ways to protect yourself before things ever reach that point.

There isn't a "right" or "wrong" way to deal with getting canceled, but there are simple actions you can take to help move you toward your goals, and there are those that end up moving you farther away. If the goal is to continue doing branded content, then maybe curating some of the online image is worth it by managing what's being said.

Don't overshare

Simply put, some things are better left unsaid. Many people, especially if they're vloggers who chronicle their daily lives, feel an incessant need to divulge every bit of information about themselves and their lives online. But the internet doesn't necessarily need to be a magnifying glass on every single aspect of your life. That's the beauty of it. No matter how many vlogs and personal stories you post, you are the editor and curator. You decide what content makes the cut.

Determining how much to share can be tricky because, of course, the more personal information you put out there, the closer your audience feels to you. That connection is a good thing! However, there needs to be a balance. Building a rapport with your viewers while keeping your views on controversial topics private can prove to be difficult for some creators. The downside of oversharing online is that you get too comfortable with revealing every intimate detail, and your thoughts and opinions might unsettle or ostracize some viewers. Of course, there will be a select few viewers that stand by you no matter what, but for the most part, even the most loyal of audiences can be swayed depending on the content you post.

Daniel Miller states, "While I'm comfortable sharing personal challenges and vulnerable moments from my life, I make a conscious effort not to overshare details involving other people. Protecting their privacy while sharing my own story has allowed me to keep boundaries with others, as most of them aren't as comfortable being on social media as I am."

Be aware of politically charged and controversial topics

Certain subjects, like politics and current events, will always offend people. Some creators manage to share their thoughts and opinions in a professional and eloquent manner, but others . . . well, not so much! Some examples of "hot button" topics include presidential elections and voting, abortion/reproductive rights, immigration and border control, gender roles, LGBTQ+ issues, racism, gun control, climate change, healthcare, economic inequality, free speech, education, criminal justice, religion, and AI.

Of course, you probably have opinions on controversial topics, and it's tempting to share those thoughts on social media. If a topic is especially important to you and you think you can do some good by posting about it, you do you! But just remember that if you openly voice a strong opinion on "hot button" topics, you risk getting hate comments and being canceled.

Do some damage control

You might be asking, when will the scandal and negative comments blow over? How long will it take? Truthfully, it depends on how badly canceled you are. Nikki Phillippi's dog euthanasia debacle seemed to blow over after she micromanaged comments, disabled comments on Instagram, and took a hiatus from social media. In a year's time, it seemed like most people had forgotten about the scandal.

If you do post something that doesn't land well, you could respond in the same way Nikki did. That silence worked in her favor. Talking about the scandal too much only gives it more energy. After being dropped from her brand deals, she briefly addressed the controversy in a Q&A-style video about how she'd grown from it, but she didn't go into much detail about how it affected her brand collaborations. That seems to be the best move when you post something you can't take back. Step away for a bit, then return to creating content once you feel ready.

While audiences may not forget, the overwhelming majority of people will eventually move onto something else, especially if there isn't much activity keeping the controversy alive. If you constantly bring it up, respond to every comment, or act like your career is over, people are more likely to stay fixated on it. Try to move on in a way that makes sense to you, whether that means blocking people, turning off comments, deleting posts that make you uncomfortable, or simply choosing to ignore it all. Damage control doesn't have to be dramatic. What matters is that your plan is achievable and long-lasting.

Write a statement rather than appear on video

People really underutilize the power of the written word. Public statements, apologies, and announcements don't require you to sit in front of the camera looking teary-eyed and gloomy. In fact, those apologies are the ones that typically get ripped apart the most. Making a video exposes you to people overanalyzing everything from your body language, to what you're wearing, to the background. This is a particularly vulnerable time for you as a creator. The chips are down, and you're riding out a low point. Don't give the haters more ammunition to use against you.

Take some time to process

It's so important to move through this space with clarity. Every post, every comment, every reaction can feel personal and permanent. But before you respond emotionally, take a beat. Think about your long-term goals and what you need to do to move forward. The clearer and more levelheaded about a situation you can be, the better off you'll be. Maybe instead of responding to a hate comment, you let it sit for a day and decide whether you want to respond to it tomorrow. Taking time and space to reflect and decide what you want to do often yields a far more desirable result than jumping the gun and making a rash move.

Prepare to defend your content

We started doing this thing in private where we would practice defending our content to each other. We would envision someone who was a professional in the industry asking us about our sponsorship and why we chose to do it. We would then discuss what we'd say to that person and how we would defend our very hard-earned deals. For example, "We accepted a sponsorship from this mobile gaming app because we both genuinely enjoy playing the game and worked hard to unlock new levels," or "Marissa has had products from that brand in her Amazon Subscribe & Save orders for over five years."

We're not saying you need to defend every single piece of content you ever post. But for us, getting past the fears of being canceled meant talking it out with each other and standing by our decision to do things like sponsored content.

Now, if you create content about more controversial topics, like politics, race, gender, or ethnicity, then you will most likely have to deal with a larger scale of hate comments. However, if you create more curated, family-friendly content and feel nervous about getting too much hate, think about what you would say to someone in your personal life who started criticizing you for a video you posted. If you can defend your content in a rational way that makes sense to you, then go ahead and post it.

But Is All Press Good Press?

The old saying goes, "all press is good press." The idea is that even negative attention keeps your name in circulation, sparks conversations, and builds awareness where silence might have left you invisible. Publicity—good or bad—reminds people you exist, and sometimes even criticism can draw in curious supporters or strengthen your loyal base. So if the goal is to have the most viewers and get the most ad revenue possible, then maybe it is worth it to leave hate comments to stir up drama.

Some people revel in the hate comments and use them for content, others respond to every single comment with something sassy or witty, and few creators will feel the need to delete every single hate comment and pretend they never existed. Some will move on immediately and resume posting. Others will take a few weeks or even months off to let things simmer down. The important thing to realize, however, is that none of these solutions is "right" or "wrong." But at the end of the day, not every headline is worth the toll it takes. Publicity only has value if it aligns with what you stand for. You must do what is right for your brand, your values, and your mental health. Staying true to yourself builds a foundation that no fleeting buzz can replace.

Returning to social media after being canceled requires a lot of personal discretion. This may mean changing up your content, depending on what happened. In some cases, completely pivoting your content may be helpful. For example, if you were a comedy creator that audiences and brands found offensive, you might want to shift away from continuing the content that others felt was problematic.

PART 3

Running Your Business

11

Sources of Revenue

Money, money, money!

Let's be real. Most people decide to become influencers because they hope to make a lot of money doing something they enjoy.

There's no need to play coy or act like money doesn't matter to you. Of course it matters! You're putting in the work because you want something tangible in return. And that something is income.

Internal validation is great and all, but it doesn't pay your rent or cover your shopping habit. Whether you're approaching social media as a hobby you squeeze in on weekends or with the discipline and dedication of a second job, you should always be thinking of monetization.

In this chapter, we highlight ways you can earn money from the content you post on social media. While many influencers pursue brand deals, there are other viable options. We're here to give you fresh ideas and inspiration!

Diversification: Don't Put All Your Eggs in One Basket

Depending on just one platform or just one form of income is risky. Algorithms change. Monetization rules shift. We've seen it before. One minute you're thriving, and the next, an update knocks your reach in half.

To avoid "having all your eggs in one basket," you need to diversify your income. That means you're not just relying on one paycheck to support your career. It's about spreading out your income streams so that if one slows down or disappears, you're not stuck.

In the creator economy, you can't afford to rely on brand deals alone. Budgets get paused, priorities shift, and the income you earn from campaigns can swing from amazing to nonexistent. If this is your only source of revenue, you're putting yourself in a vulnerable position. The more you diversify, the less your income depends on an algorithm or a company's marketing budget.

Diversification isn't about doing everything; it's about finding what works for you. There's no one-size-fits-all path here. Just a lot of options and opportunities waiting to be tapped into. The more you explore, the more freedom you create for yourself.

Brandi Marie King, an actress and lifestyle influencer who frequently turns up on Hollywood red carpets, says, "My biggest tip for new creators is to stay flexible and adaptable because this industry can change at any time. Don't rely too heavily on just one platform.

"I started my influencer career on Vine, which was a platform where you could post really short videos that were only six seconds long. In 2017, the app shut down for good. Pretty much overnight, I had to start over again on all new platforms with zero followers. It was challenging to transition to making longer content. At first, I wondered, 'How am I going to fill up a whole fifteen seconds?' Thankfully, I was able to make the transition!"

We used to go to a lot of business building workshops at YouTube Space in Los Angeles, and people were constantly talking about income diversification in a way that would get on our nerves. We'd get annoyed because it seemed like such a meaningless buzzword. People would constantly tell you that you should be doing it, and it was bad if you didn't do it, but they never had anything practical to say about *how* to diversify your income. How do you find the time to do that? How can you possibly set up another income stream when you're already spending so much of your time creating content?

If you don't build the business side, no one will

A common mistake influencers make is treating content creation like the entire job and ignoring the business that actually supports it. When people imagine doing social media professionally, they picture the fun parts: brainstorming ideas, shaping the aesthetic, filming, editing, and posting. What they do not picture is the unglamorous side of the job: emails, admin, and logistics. No one loves that work, but it is part of the deal if you want to move forward.

If you pour all your time into creating and none into running the business, your growth will hit a ceiling. It is hard to accept that you also need to add more work on top of creating content, especially the boring and uncreative parts. But that is the reality of turning content creation into a real career. If you're struggling to find the time to diversify and monetize your content, you might want to consider finding someone you trust to help you. That person doesn't have to be an agent or manager. It could be a friend, a sibling, a classmate, or even a virtual assistant. The key is that they understand your goals and can handle things well. You have to learn how to outsource and delegate if you want to grow. Trying to do everything on your own will burn you out, especially as your business expands. We found that having a duo helped a lot, but you can absolutely do it on your own if you stay focused and intentional.

Building the business side takes real effort. It will not magically happen on its own. You have to carve out time to think about income streams and how to scale. Yes, it would be great if someone just swooped in and did it all for you, but this is your career. Whether you team up with someone or do it solo, the important thing is to take it seriously. Otherwise, it's never going to get off the ground.

The Truth About Passive Income

Let's clear something up. Passive income is never truly passive. People love the idea of making money in their sleep, and yes, that can happen, but there is still work involved. Setting up those systems takes effort. Whether you are launching a course or building a product line, you must continually update, improve, and explore new ways to keep your audience engaged. For example, if you have a course, you're going to need to update it and add new offerings to sell to your existing customers. If you have a product, you're going to have to introduce new colors or designs, flavors, or scents. You're obviously going to continue innovating and creating new ways to sell to your audience. Nothing runs itself forever!

Find a balance

It is better to do a few things really well than to spread yourself thin by working on too many projects that never fully take off. Each income stream requires attention, strategy, and upkeep. Quality always wins over quantity. It sounds cool to say you have ten revenue streams, but if each of those makes $100 per year, well, that's not much, is it? It's often more effective to focus on just a few forms of income that perform well.

Estrella Serrato, a podcast host, says, "Looking back, I was diversifying before I even knew what that meant. About six months after I started, someone from Cal State Channel Islands invited me to give a keynote speech. That moment made me realize I could actually talk about this work in a meaningful way. After that, I started getting three to five speaking gigs a year, all while being a full-time student. Later, I saw firsthand how unpredictable brand deals can be. They come in waves, which meant I had to get serious about building more stable income streams. That's when I launched my mentorship program for college students, started selling merch, and took on consulting work with universities."

It may seem like a lot of work up front, but when a video goes viral, or sales start rolling in, you will be glad you took the time to build your revenue streams thoughtfully and strategically. Just remember, not every piece of content should be pushing a product. People can tell when they are being sold to. Focus on creating real value through education, entertainment, or both, and the sales will follow.

Ways to Build Revenue Streams on Social Media

There are countless ways to earn income through social media today, and the landscape continues to evolve at a rapid pace. New platforms, tools, and startups are constantly emerging, each introducing fresh opportunities for creators to monetize their presence and expertise. The examples that follow only scratch the surface, but they'll give you a sense of the many possible paths. If one of these sparks your interest, it's worth doing some research to determine if it's a good option for you and your content.

Ad revenue

If you use platforms like YouTube, TikTok, or Facebook, you can make money just by posting. Their ad programs pay you for views and engagement. There are always minimum requirements creators must hit to qualify for monetization, requirements that change from time to time. For example, in 2025, YouTube required the account to have 1,000 subscribers and 4,000 hours of watch time in the past twelve months.

Each platform handles ad revenue a little differently. At its core, ad revenue rewards creators for holding people's attention. The longer viewers stay on the platform engaging with your content, the more ad inventory the platform can sell, and the more you can earn in return.

Affiliate marketing

Affiliate marketing is when a creator shares a specific link to a product or service and earns a small commission when their viewers buy the product using the shared link.

You recommend something you love, someone buys it through your link, and you get a cut. That's it. Easy. Tools like Amazon Associates, ShopMy, or LIKEtoKNOW.It (LTK) make it easy to share links. The more trust you build with your audience, the more you'll earn from their clicks. It's a way to make money by recommending things you like without having to create or sell the product yourself. We personally love shopping on Amazon and order several new things each week. Sharing our favorite tooth whitening strips or acne stickers with our followers feels like telling friends about a little treasure we found. It is fun and effortless.

Branded merchandise

If you have a strong aesthetic or a catchphrase your followers love, consider turning it into merch—products like t-shirts, hoodies, hats, or mugs featuring your name, logo, or designs. You can use print-on-demand services to eliminate the need for inventory management.

Physical products

Go beyond merch and build a real product line. Maybe it's a skincare brand, a candle collection, journals, or your own coffee blend. This option is more complex than merch, but it can become a major part of your brand. Take Marianna Hewitt, for example. She turned her online audience into a thriving skincare brand called Summer Fridays. Today, her products are sold in Sephora and stand on their own, beyond her identity as a content creator.

Anastasia St. John, who runs an online vintage clothing store called Amethyst Lullabies, says, "I use social media to market my business by creating content that highlights my best pieces in beautiful photos or short-form videos. This strategy enables me to showcase my aesthetic and get people excited about new releases from my vintage shop!"

Anastasia uses her posts to capture the attention of a niche audience passionate about vintage pieces. "I do feel like social media has helped my brand grow. My brand would not be what it is today without the extra boost from my posts. It helps reach my correct target audience of vintage collectors and enthusiasts while also creating a demand for new pieces and brings in a steady flow of new customers."

Digital products

This is where your creativity can shine. Digital products are files you create and sell online that people can download or access instantly. You make them once, and then you can sell them over and over, making them a great source of passive income. Plus, digital products don't need to be shipped, so you don't need to worry about carrying inventory!

There is a wide variety of digital products you can create depending on your skills and audience. Some popular options include photo or video presets, design templates, eBooks, Notion planners, online courses, or downloadable art and illustrations. You can also create guides, workbooks, music, stock photos, or digital patterns for crafting and design.

Social media can be an excellent way to consistently attract new buyers. When deciding where to sell your digital products, consider the platforms that match your audience and the type of product you are offering. Platforms like Instagram and TikTok make it easy to showcase your products in action, build excitement, and drive traffic directly to your shop.

Paid subscriptions

Paid subscriptions are when your audience pays a monthly or yearly fee to get exclusive content or perks from you. It's a great way to earn steady income while giving your biggest fans something extra. You can offer behind-the-scenes content, early access, bonus posts, or a private community. Platforms like Patreon, Substack, Ko-fi, or Instagram Subscriptions help your audience support you directly.

Services

If you're skilled in areas such as photography, design, editing, or coaching, turn that talent into a service! You can freelance for brands, consult with other creators, or build a side business that runs alongside your content.

UGC (User-Generated Content) for brands

UGC is when brands pay creators to take photos, film videos, or create other content that the brand can use to promote its products. Since the content is posted on the brand's accounts, you don't need to have a big following. If you don't want to fill your feed with sponsored content but still want to work with brands and have strong content creation skills, this can be a great option.

Speaking gigs and panels

As your platform grows, people will start seeing you as an expert in your field. That can lead to paid speaking opportunities, podcast interviews, panel invites, or even teaching a workshop.

Licensing your content

Sometimes a brand or media outlet wants to use a photo, video, or audio clip you already made, maybe in a paid advertisement, on their website or social media page, or even in a movie or TV show. Since you own the content, they'll pay you for a license that allows them to use it. You don't need to do any extra work!

Personalized video shoutouts

Apps like Cameo let fans pay for customized videos of you. You can wish someone a happy birthday, give advice, or even do a fun roast. If people love your personality, they'll pay to get a little piece of it.

Live-streaming for tips

When you go live, your audience can send you virtual gifts or tips in real time. Twitch, TikTok Live, YouTube, and Instagram all have features that let fans show their support in dollars.

Social media management for others

Not every business owner wants to run their own social media. That's where you come in. Local businesses, such as dentist offices or fitness studios, will pay for someone to create, edit, and post content regularly. You already know how to make content work, so why not do it for others, too?

Going on tour/in-person meet and greets

One exciting way to expand your brand is by connecting with your online followers in real life. This approach is growing in popularity and offers a unique way to turn digital relationships into personal experiences. Many popular podcasts host live shows or tours in different cities, where fans can buy tickets and meet the hosts in person. Fitness influencers bring their followers together for live workout classes or interactive workshops. These events allow followers to experience the community you have built online in a tangible way and often create deeper connections with your audience.

Beyond shows and tours, creators can host private meetups, fan conventions, or even pop-up events tailored to their niche. These opportunities not only provide a new source of income but also make your brand more memorable and give your audience a chance to interact with you in new ways.

Tom Ward, an industry insider who has worked both in front of the camera and behind the scenes, has interviewed a whole roster of top influencers and celebrities for *Forbes* magazine, including Paris Hilton, Jake Paul, Logan Paul, Tana Mongeau, Kate Hudson, and others. He now works in the podcasting space. He believes that the future of social media is going to move to in-person activations. "I predict that the future of social media will be IRL (in real life) events. You can get followers online, but can you get them out of their house in real life to a pop-up event for your brand, or on a tour with a meet and greet? The trend will be to see social media spill into real life."

When to Start Monetizing

One mistake many creators make, of which we are certainly guilty, is not focusing on monetization right from the start. We firmly believe that you should have several monetization strategies (ideally four or five) in place from the very beginning, even if those strategies change over time as you gain experience.

One big, big mistake is thinking "I have to build my audience huge first before I start monetizing!"

You are missing out on money and leaving opportunities on the table if you do that. Your audience numbers will fluctuate. You want to have those revenue streams in place for when you unexpectedly go viral, rather than trying to come up with something to sell when the audience's interest is already starting to wane.

Don't make the same mistake we made! We delayed implementing monetization strategies, and by the time we released products our audience liked, interest in them was fading.

When to Start Monetizing

12

Working with Brands

Working with brands is one of the most popular and lucrative ways influencers make money. It can also be really nuanced and difficult to navigate. That's why we've dedicated this whole chapter to the ins and outs of constructively collaborating with brands.

In this chapter, we discuss best practices for attracting a brand's attention and securing a deal, walk you through how to reach out to your dream brand to propose a deal, and share advice regarding what to do when problems occur. You're on your way to achieving what you might not have thought possible: working with influential companies that sell products you love.

Securing Inbound Brand Deals

When we refer to inbound versus outbound brand deals, what we mean is "Did the brand reach out to you first (inbound) or did you reach out to them first (outbound or outreach)?"

Influencer life is way easier when brands reach out to you first. Imagine opening your inbox and seeing an email from a brand, asking about your rates, or even better, offering you a specific amount. Now that's what we call a great day!

If you have a "healthy inbound," it means that a lot of brands want to work with you. If they find you and make you an offer, most of the work has already been done. All that's left is to negotiate the terms of the deal, hammer out the fine print in a contract, and *boom.* Having a healthy inbound doesn't just make life easier; it also puts you in a better position to negotiate a better deal (read: more money).

However, don't think you can build a lucrative business by solely relying on inbound offers. Inbound offers are out of your control. You can wish, hope, and pray every day that Coca-Cola reaches out and offers to work with you, but odds are, it'll never happen. The world of social media is highly saturated, and simply wishing for your dream brand to reach out to you isn't realistic. We have always found it to be more effective to take control by reaching out to brands ourselves.

That being said, there are certainly things you can do to set yourself up for success and increase the likelihood of receiving those coveted inbound offers.

Optimize your bios with keywords

Think of your bio as your elevator pitch. Include keywords that reflect your niche, such as "beauty creator," "mom of twins," "LA-based foodie," or "tech reviewer." The more specific, the better. Sprinkle those same keywords in your captions, video descriptions, even your pinned posts. Brands are searching for creators, so help them find you.

Don't forget to include your location! So many brand campaigns are location-specific. If they're looking for creators in Atlanta or the Pacific Northwest or within ten miles of a pop-up event, and you haven't said where you're based, you're invisible to them. So add your city or region somewhere obvious, like in your bio or "About" section.

Put your email address on everything

Years ago, we befriended a creator who posted amazing travel content. When several of his videos went viral, we felt like proud parents! But then we noticed that he didn't have his email address written anywhere! The next time we spoke to him, we lightly scolded him, explaining that he should include his email address in his videos. There's no telling what kinds of opportunities he could've been missing out on! He was getting significant attention, but any brands that were interested in working with him didn't have a way of contacting him.

You want your email address to be easy to find so no one has to go searching for it. Make sure it's a relatively easy email address, not something where a lowercase letter could be mistaken for a number (like "L" and the number 1) or something along those lines. We're fans of simple, professional email addresses that have letters instead of numbers. Something like shanna184749202@gmail.com is easy to mistype or copy incorrectly.

Finally, it doesn't matter if you use a free email service provider like Gmail or Yahoo, instead of an email with a custom domain (or "vanity email") that you pay for. Truly, no one will judge. We used to think that people would take us more seriously and consider us more professional if we paid for a vanity email. But we've come to the conclusion that the only thing that matters is having an email address that is simple and readable.

Post brand-friendly content

Create posts that look like they could be sponsored, even if they're not. Brands love seeing how you'd organically feature their product.

For example, if you love skincare, make reels that show your routine, tag your favorite brands, and use crisp visuals. Creating content that shows up at the top of your target brand's search results is a great way to get noticed.

Organically interact with the brands you want to work with

Make it easy for your favorite brands to find you. Follow them! Like and comment on their posts! Feature their products organically in your content and always, always, always tag them! On Instagram, you can either make the tag visible to everyone, or you can choose to hide the tag so it's invisible to everyone except the brand. We sometimes use invisible tags when we want the brand to see our content, but we don't want to give them "free promo" by shouting them out to our audience.

Pro tip: when tagging brands, do so during standard business hours (Monday through Friday, 9 AM to 5 PM). Why? Because the people working for brands are regular employees who go home at the end of the day. If you tag or message the brand on a weekend or late at night, you may get an automated away message, which can make it easy for your content to slip through the cracks.

Some brands operate internationally and work across different time zones, so business hours may seem irrelevant. Still, it's good to be aware of the time differences and standard business hours for the region.

Get noticed by PR agencies

It's crucial to make connections with PR agencies because they handle many influencer deals. This might be even more important than reaching out to brands. A brand is just one single opportunity, but a PR agency represents many brands. The goal is to get added to those coveted outreach lists for campaigns, events, and gifted opportunities. Once you get on the PR agency's radar, they will contact you whenever they have an opportunity that could be a good fit.

With agencies, first impressions matter. You want to impress them the first time they work with you. We recommend going above and beyond by being professional and having a positive attitude so that they want to continue working with you.

Doing small things like purchasing flowers or an edible arrangement for the office after you execute a brand deal with a PR agency can build relationships and create a sense of loyalty. We're not saying to overly kiss up to the agency employees, but showing your appreciation can go a long way in this industry, where influencers can sometimes be perceived as entitled and ungrateful. If you get invited to a cool event, something as simple as sending a thank-you email can help you stand out. Everyone likes to be acknowledged for their hard work—even those working behind the scenes.

It's also smart to share screenshots or a link to the content you created for the event or product with your contact. This saves them time, supports the metrics they're responsible for, and makes them look good internally. It also makes them more inclined to work with you again because there's a clear record of how you showcased the brand. That way, the next time you contact them, you can refer to the solid content you made last time.

Also, be friendly with a few different employees in case your contact ends up leaving the company. PR and marketing firms often have a high turnover rate, and employees usually rotate positions a bit. Visit the office in person, if possible, and try to make a personal connection.

Showcase strong metrics

Brands seek creators with genuine influence. So show your worth by regularly sharing case studies or highlighting analytics, like engagement rate, saves, link clicks, or reach, via stories or pinned posts.

Consider creating a "Media Kit" highlight on Instagram or a pinned post on TikTok that showcases stats and prior collaborations.

Go viral (for a positive reason)

It seems obvious, but yes, going viral can help you get discovered by brands. As long as you've gone viral for the right reasons and not because of some horrible scandal, this can definitely make brands want to work with you.

Brand Outreach

When it comes to working with brands, proactive outreach is vital. While the allure of brands reaching out to you first is enticing, waiting passively for the phone to ring isn't very effective. And while it may be tempting to delegate this task to a manager or agent (see chapter 15 for details on working with these partners), the reality is that success in this arena demands personal investment. As your influence grows, you may consider outsourcing this responsibility, but in the early stages, it's essential to take ownership of your brand outreach efforts.

For lifestyle creators like ourselves, branded campaigns are the most lucrative avenue for generating income on social media. While money is just one measure of success, it is a very important metric.

Throughout our social media journey, we have collaborated with well over 300 brands. While serendipity led to a handful of these opportunities finding us first, the lion's share was the result of our proactive pursuit and diligent efforts in reaching out to brands first.

Brand outreach takes time. It requires you to be proactive, and, yes, it is usually tougher than just answering an email that pops into your inbox. But it really does work like a numbers game, where steady, focused effort pays off. If your dream brand is something huge like Coca-Cola, of course, the ideal situation is that they contact you first. Most of the time, though, you will be the one trying to figure out who the right PR person is and sending the pitch yourself, and that can feel like searching for a needle in a haystack. The good news is that when you identify which brands you want to work with and develop strong pitching habits, outreach becomes a lot more exciting. It can open the door to real opportunities and help move your creator career forward in a big way.

Monetizing your platform bears resemblance to working on a sales team, where lead generation drives commission-based earnings. Yet, while pursuing brand deals is akin to prospecting for sales, it's essential to strike a balance between the amount of time spent doing outreach and the time spent creating content. Efficiency is key, and you certainly don't want to exhaust all your time on outreach.

The first step is the most important, as well as the most time-consuming: curating a selection of brand leads. With thousands of content creators vying for online attention, it's imperative to focus your efforts on the brands that are most likely to engage with you.

Analyze your competitors' partnerships

One tried-and-true tactic is to target brands that are already collaborating with influencers within your niche. If the brand is working with other influencers, that means they have a budget for, and actively work with, creators like you. That's valuable insight!

While finding exact competitors may prove challenging, aim for creators who share thematic similarities. Remember, differences in appearance or location don't preclude relevance. Focus on creators closely aligned with your content style. For instance, if you operate in the beauty/fashion sphere, studying car creators' collaborations is counterproductive. Obviously, no one is an exact replica of another creator. But it's helpful to keep your finger on the pulse of who is working with whom.

Fortunately, our natural inclination to scroll through social media feeds can serve as a valuable tool in this endeavor. Start paying attention to whom these similar creators are working with. Take note of when they disclose sponsored content with hashtags like #ad or #sponsored. That's invaluable market research.

We personally like to screenshot the #ad posts we see our competition posting. Once or twice a week, we review the screenshots and contact those brands one at a time, ensuring that we aren't waiting months before contacting a potential lead. Timing matters a lot when it comes to brands and their budgets. When you notice a brand working with other influencers, it's good to contact them right away.

Identify brands with influencer budgets

Focus on companies that actually have the budgets to fairly pay creators. Typically, startups and small companies with limited staff boast smaller budgets, making them less conducive to lucrative collaborations. We like to aim for mid-sized brands with 50 to 150 employees. This is just a general guideline, though, not a hard-and-fast rule.

To pinpoint brands with the means to pay social media influencers, use resources like Crunchbase, which shares valuable data insight into companies with newfound financial backing.

It's also a good idea to look into a brand's history of influencer partnerships to gauge their budget. How many creators are they hiring? Is it just one or two, or are they booking numerous creators for their campaigns? Do a little bit of your own research. That way, if a brand claims to have absolutely no budget, but they've hired a dozen similar creators to you in the past month, then you know they're just trying to get away with giving you free product in exchange for video content. Brands often push boundaries, seeking to maximize their returns. By conducting thorough research, you're equipped to navigate negotiations with clarity and confidence.

Target your dream brands

Don't be afraid to think outside the box! Who do you really, really want to work with? We know this might seem to contradict the advice to stay in your lane and do what your competitors are doing, and while aligning with your niche is advisable, it's also worthwhile to be a bit ambitious.

Pursue partnerships that resonate with your personal passions, even if they seem unrelated to your content.

Take, for instance, our unexpected journey with the legendary rock band Queen. Most people wouldn't guess just by looking at us that we're huge Queen fans. Despite our content not being overtly related to music or film, our deep admiration for Queen inspired us to reach out to the PR team at 20th Century Fox behind the 2018 movie *Bohemian Rhapsody*. We wrote a short email saying we were fans and expressing our interest in being involved in promoting the film.

This "shot in the dark" led to an extraordinary opportunity. We attended the press tour, took a private jet to Las Vegas with the cast of the film, saw the band perform up close (we were in the third row!), and even got to meet two of the original band members. To our disbelief, we were not only invited on the press tour but also generously compensated for this once-in-a-lifetime experience. We never imagined we'd get to have such an incredible experience, much less get paid to do it.

Similarly, our love for theme parks unexpectedly opened doors for our business. Growing up in Southern California, we've always been obsessed with theme parks. Though it's embarrassing to confess, we are, undeniably, "Disney adults."

However, we rarely made content involving theme parks, focusing instead on beauty, fashion, and women's health. Even though Disney content was not our niche, our love of all things Disney inspired us to contact theme park companies. It took a few tries to find the right employees and the correct email addresses (more on how to do this later), but we eventually were able to connect, resulting in years of complimentary tickets and unique VIP experiences worth thousands of dollars to Disneyland, Walt Disney World, Universal Studios, Knott's Berry Farm, and more. We eventually turned our Disney connections into a paid brand deal, as well as a complimentary trip across the country to Walt Disney World. Not every partnership will result in monetary compensation, but the value of free products or experiences aligned with your passions should not be underestimated.

In our experience, local, experience-based opportunities often prove to be the most accessible, especially to smaller creators. With a product, anything can be mailed to a creator around the country or even the world, depending on where the product is sold. But for an experience, the brand typically needs someone local, resulting in a smaller pool of potential collaborators. If you have enthusiasm, you're professional, you reach out to the right people, and you make their jobs easy, there's a good chance you'll be successful. By identifying unique angles that resonate with brands, even seemingly unrelated partnerships can flourish, yielding high-value rewards.

So ask yourself: What are you into? What do you find fun? Are you a food vlogger but need some new furniture for your house? Do you post about parenting but have been dreaming about some new tech gadget?

You can post a one-off piece of content and find a way to tie it in! For example, the food vlogger requesting furniture might use the content in a video that provides a behind-the-scenes tour of their workspace. The parent who wants a tech gadget might incorporate it into a post called "Fun gift ideas for Father's Day!"

You might be afraid that it will have lower viewership than the content your audience knows you for, but that's not necessarily the case. It could also prove to be an opportunity. For example, our theme park content exceeded our expectations by performing much better than we anticipated. It turns out that our audience liked that content as well, and we were able to incorporate more of it into our future content. Even if it gets fewer views, you can weigh the trade-offs of doing something you really want and fulfilling a goal or dream.

If you don't reach out and ask, you'll never know what can happen. We are firm believers that authentic passion can transcend traditional boundaries and open doors to remarkable opportunities.

With your meticulously curated list of brands in hand, it's time to embark on the trickier task of initiating contact. Here's where the real finesse comes into play.

In our next section we'll discuss exactly how to get in contact with a brand you want to work with. How do you know who to contact and how do you find the correct employee's email address? There are different strategies, from sending direct messages to the brand's Instagram or TikTok account, to finding Influencer Marketing Manager employees on LinkedIn and sourcing their email addresses, to connecting with PR agencies who are often the gatekeepers to marketing budgets.

The power of a well-crafted message

Armed with your curated list of potential brands, you are now ready to initiate contact. We attribute a lot of our success to sending good messages. We think messages should be short and to the point.

In today's day and age, the best way to connect with a brand you want to work with is over social media DM, usually on Instagram or TikTok. It's easy, it's fast, it's direct. You don't have to waste a couple hours of your time working on it. You can find a brand's page and send a message in a few minutes. The purpose of sending the DM is to communicate your interest in working with the brand as efficiently as possible, and then move that conversation to email, which is a more professional way of communication.

Communicating via social media direct message (DM)

A surprising number of brands prefer to conduct brand deals over DM. Shanna worked out a deal like this when she was planning her wedding. She was looking for a second dress to wear to her reception dinner—something shorter and more casual. She kept getting Instagram ads from this one particular brand with the most gorgeous, short, sparkly wedding dress. She decided to shoot her shot and send the brand a DM over Instagram.

> Hi there,
>
> I'd love to get in touch about promoting your dresses to my audience! I am a bride-to-be, and I have a YouTube channel with 1.6+ million subscribers. Is there a PR contact email you can pass along?
>
> Best,
>
> Shanna

The brand responded by asking for more details about the kind of promotion she could offer in exchange for the dress. Shanna suggested talking about the dress in a long-form YouTube video for two minutes and posting a photo of herself wearing it on Instagram. She also added that she was open to hearing the brand's ideas as far as promotion went. Shanna told them which dress she preferred and also mentioned a few others she liked. This was a strategic decision because it let the brand know that if they couldn't gift her the dress she really loved, she was still open to working with them and would accept a different dress as compensation. This showed the brand she's flexible.

Shanna ended up conducting the whole transaction via Instagram DM and never moved conversation to email.

By the way, Shanna looked fabulous in the dress and felt like a movie star!

Communicating via email

Finding the right email address can be difficult, but it isn't impossible. You can often find a brand's contact info on their website or on a press release. There also might be a media/inquiry form on the company site that you can fill out. Whether this is for a branded deal, tickets to something, an affiliate deal, or just for free product, it's always a good idea to just fill it out. Even though this is obviously the least personal way, sometimes it's simply the quickest way to get things done.

Our least favorite, most time-consuming, and most difficult way to track down a PR contact is on LinkedIn. Basically, you type into Google something like "LinkedIn (Company Name)" and then some variation of "Public Relations." Job titles can differ depending on the company. Sometimes the appropriate contact is in a role called "Influencer Marketing Manager," "PR Manager," "Digital Social Media Manager," or something else. Read the person's job description and see if they work with influencers on paid campaigns. There might be a few employees to choose from. If that's the case, then you have to decide whether to go with the person who has been at the company longer (and has more experience) or the person who is newer (and has more to prove and might be more open to working with you).

Then of course, there is the annoying task of actually finding the person's email address, if it isn't included on their profile. Back to Google. Search (Company Name) email address format. Most company email addresses are variations of firstname.lastname@company.com, firstinitiallastname@company.com, or firstname@company.com, and so on. Sometimes you guess, send it off, and the email bounces right back saying it does not exist, which means you have to rewind and try again. (Do you see why we prefer DM?)

Drafting your outreach message

When you cold message a brand employee to propose a collaboration (and ask for money) you must be extremely professional. No typos. No mistakes. You want to quickly and effectively communicate who you are and why you are contacting them. We genuinely believe that the reason we've had so much success with emails is that we have mastered this skill.

Here is an example of an initial outreach message:

> Hi there, *(A person's name is best! But if you don't know it, "Hi there" is totally fine.)*
>
> I'm a fashion content creator with 200K Instagram followers. *(Brag about yourself! We like to name our most impressive fact right off the bat. Maybe that's your follower number, but maybe not. Maybe it's some achievement. Try to make it something numerical.)*
>
> I'm reaching out because I'd love to incorporate your product into a sponsored video on ______. *(Get to the point. Don't beat around the bush. Explain exactly what you want. Also, give a specific example of what you want to put it in.)*
>
> Thank you! Looking forward to hearing from you!
>
> Best,
> Shanna

You should also include links to your websites or social media profiles at the bottom of your email. If you're sending a DM via social media, links aren't necessary.

If you don't receive a reply within about a week, try following up. Here's an example of a follow-up message:

Hi Kaitlin,

Happy Monday! Following up on my previous email! Let me know if you'd like to work together to promote SillyBounce to my audience!

Best,
Shanna

Note how the follow-up email is short, sweet, and to the point. Follow-ups should also provide the recipient with a reminder of what the initial message was about.

Best Practices

Working with brands might look simple from the outside, but there's a real art to managing a brand deal from start to finish. Brands come in all shapes and sizes, so in this section we share some essential tips to help you build long-term, sustainable success. You'll learn how to present yourself professionally, meet tough deadlines, and navigate tricky situations with confidence. These are the skills that help turn one-time deals into lasting partnerships.

We'll also talk through real-world scenarios you might encounter if you stick with brand partnerships long enough.

Get it in writing

We'll give it to you straight. When working with brands, you're bound to encounter *some* kind of issue at one point or another. Oftentimes, when problems arise, brands request phone calls. In this scenario, we recommend redirecting the conversation back to email. Many brands use phone calls to try to convince influencers to do things their way or ask for additional favors and promotion. Avoid putting yourself in a situation where you could be pushed around. More importantly, use email to create a paper trail of the communication.

When we had a legal dispute with a laser hair removal company, the brand repeatedly asked for phone call after phone call. We responded that for legal purposes we needed everything to be in writing—a decision that proved to be a good one since we eventually had to take legal action against them.

The only time we recommend having a phone call is when the brand is deciding whether they want to hire you or not, or if you're currently doing a deal and the brand is looking to discuss additional creative ideas, which can be difficult to brainstorm over email.

Communicate proactively

A little communication goes a very long way. Let brands know when they can expect you to complete the work you agreed to do. If you need an extra day or two, say you're "putting the finishing touches on editing." This is a completely understandable reason for the delay! Everyone knows editing takes a long time and can be quite tedious. Most brands will typically be fine with this as long as there isn't a super strict deadline.

When you know you aren't going to hit a deadline, communicate that with the brand right away. Don't wait until the deadline to let them know you'll be late. Letting them know in advance is respectful and gives the brand the opportunity to prepare accordingly.

Keep calm and stay professional

Sometimes brand employees don't treat influencers with professionalism and respect. It's important to use discretion with brands and to know when to push back and when to accommodate a brand you want to work with again. The vital thing to understand is that there's no real right or wrong way to fully execute a brand deal; however, there are actions that help you yield the results you want, and actions that don't help you achieve your goals. As tempting as it might be to send a sassy or emotional email, it's best to keep things polite and professional. A brand might complain that your content didn't perform well enough, send you a hostile email demanding more posts, or even claim that your file attachment crashed their computer. We've been in all of those situations before. It's important to remain calm and professional even if a brand doesn't reciprocate that professionalism. That's how you achieve your goal and win the long game.

Get the work done, no matter what

Brands can sometimes want what seems impossible, like a super tight deadline or a bunch of additional rounds of edits that weren't agreed on. Companies often want the most bang for their buck, and many will have no problem asking for additional free posts, giveaways, whitelisting (this is where a brand runs ads directly through an influencer's account), reuploading rights, and other perks for which they should really pay more.

Even though there are definitely situations when you should set firm boundaries or even walk away from a deal, there are other times when a different approach might be necessary. When you are working with a successful brand that is paying you well, sometimes you have to do whatever it takes to get the project done.

Working with brands will not always go smoothly, even when the deal is big and the relationship is strong. We once ran a major campaign with a large corporation during which communication completely broke down. After we filmed and edited the entire video, the brand unexpectedly sent a list of changes and then told us the revised draft had to be done within a few hours to meet their fiscal deadline. It was unrealistic and frustrating, and our first instinct was to push back. Instead, we chose to stay calm, reshoot the video immediately, and just get it done. It was stressful, but we met the deadline and kept an important long-term relationship intact.

The takeaway for creators is simple. When problems come up, ask yourself what your real goal is before reacting. A few helpful questions are: Is this worth getting upset over? How important is this deal to me? Does pushing back help me or hurt my chances of future work? Sometimes the smartest move is to power through and deliver, especially when the brand is one you value, or the rate makes the extra effort worthwhile. On the other hand, if the pay is low and the demands are unreasonable, it might make more sense to walk away. Use good judgment, remain professional, and keep your long-term goals in mind. That will guide you toward the right call every time.

Lessons We Learned the Hard Way (So You Don't Have To)

Let's be honest—brand deals are not always a walk in the park. In this section, we share personal anecdotes about brand deals that took a turn for the worse. We reminisce on things we did right and things we definitely would've done differently if given the chance. We hope you can learn from our experiences.

Know when to walk away

When we were first starting out as creators, we booked a small $100 brand deal with a shopping app that no longer exists. The campaign seemed straightforward at first, but it quickly turned into a nightmare. After multiple phone calls, endless emails, and very unclear direction, it became obvious the brand expected far more than what was originally agreed on.

Realizing we were being taken advantage of, we sent a professional message to the brand letting them know we were stepping away from the deal. This experience taught us an early but important lesson. Some brands will try to push inexperienced creators into giving more than they signed up for, hoping they will say yes just to be agreeable. Learning when to walk away helped us set stronger boundaries moving forward and reminded us that not every deal is worth your time.

Be your own advocate

In 2022, we signed a $4,000 brand deal with a New Zealand–based company, known for their at-home laser hair removal devices. We had worked with them before and assumed this campaign would run smoothly.

After submitting the completed video around Christmas, the brand unexpectedly asked to delay the campaign until the second quarter of the year. We pushed back, explaining the timeline was not workable. What followed was months of excuses and delays. We were told the payment was delayed due to holidays, employee leave, and international banking issues. Eventually, we escalated the situation to the New Zealand

Disputes Tribunal. After a court hearing and nearly a year of chasing down our payment, we were awarded a partial settlement of approximately $2,500. While this was disappointing, it still felt like a win to finally put the matter to rest and cut ties with the brand.

This ordeal taught us that a good past experience does not guarantee a good future one. Brands change, employees change, and terms can shift unexpectedly. You have to stay sharp, read every contract carefully, and always be ready to advocate for yourself. No one will protect your business like you will.

Protect yourself by understanding your contract (and don't be afraid to get a lawyer)

In the summer of 2020, we booked a $3,500 brand deal with a self-tanning company. We submitted our analytics, signed the contract, and got to work filming content in accordance with their detailed brief. Despite a minor mix-up in product shades, we delivered a polished video ahead of schedule and made a few simple edits the brand requested. Then, out of nowhere, they asked for a full reshoot. We complied, but after weeks of vague feedback, the PR representative told us the brand was canceling the campaign, claiming it was no longer a good investment. Their "compensation" was a box of products and an invitation to their affiliate program.

We pushed back, reminding them that the contract didn't allow them to cancel after the work had been completed. They offered a fraction of the original rate and repeatedly asked to jump on a call, which we declined in favor of written communication. When we refused to accept less than we were owed, we offered a $2,500 settlement to quickly resolve things. They countered with just $600, so we involved our lawyer, who sent the brand a formal letter. Almost immediately, the brand agreed to move forward with the terms outlined in our original contract. We posted the video and finally received the full payment.

This experience taught us the value of knowing our rights and standing firm. While we always aim to work things out on our own first, some situations call for legal support. Not every disagreement can be solved through friendly emails or compromise, and when a brand breaks their agreement, it is not your job to carry the emotional burden. Sometimes the most professional thing you can do is let the contract speak for itself.

13

Navigating Freebies

When approaching brands, it's almost always best to aim for a paid deal first. If given the choice between receiving a product that retails for $50, or scoring $5,000 from a paid post, the answer seems obvious. But if the brand isn't willing to pay you, or doesn't do paid deals with any creators, period, then you might want to consider asking for or accepting a freebie, sometimes called a "thank you gift" or "complimentary merchandise." To determine if accepting a freebie as compensation is the right move, we like to ask ourselves a few questions: Is this something I actually want and will use, or will this turn into clutter? Would I spend my own money on this item anyway? Is this something nicer and more expensive than something I would buy for myself? If we still want the item, then accepting a freebie instead of a traditional payment makes sense in that situation. While free products are certainly not the same as income, they do carry value. When calculating your earnings, especially in this industry, it's important to factor in what those gifted items might be worth.

But of course, these freebies come with a catch. You've probably heard of the expression "There is no such thing as a free lunch," meaning that nothing is truly free, even if the cost is not obvious. If you accept a gift from a brand, they expect you to do something for them in return, like creating promotional content. Some brands expect you to put in more work than others, so it's important to consider whether or not that gift is worth the trouble.

In this chapter, you'll learn about asking for goods and services, navigating high-value freebies, and determining when it's better to simply walk away from a demanding brand rather than accepting a freebie.

Paid Campaigns Versus Freebies

Paid deals are significantly more difficult to get than free products and experiences. While that might seem like common knowledge, noting why is important.

Paid campaigns often come with stricter guidelines and higher expectations because when they're paying you, they expect you to put in more work. You'll often have to work with various departments, like accounting or legal, not just PR. Sometimes the brand provides a more concrete script with talking points, as well as a contract. Invoices, W9 forms, and other paperwork might be involved. We don't say this to make paid deals sound bad, because it's obviously better to earn income rather than free products or experiences. However, there are fundamental differences and expectations associated with both.

Not only can comped items be a lot easier to get, but they can provide a means for you to get things you'd never dream of spending your own money on! For example, we've been gifted thousands of dollars' worth of manicures, pedicures, hair/makeup services, theme park tickets/experiences, tickets to various shows/plays/musicals, and other amazing experiences—all things we'd never consider buying with our own money.

Freebie Etiquette

If you are on a PR list and regularly receive unsolicited gifts in the mail, or if a brand reaches out to you first, offering to send something your way, there are generally no mandatory obligations to post about it unless otherwise stated. But when you reach out to a brand to ask for something for free, there is an implicit understanding that you will post promotional content about it. You might suggest filming a collaborative reel on Instagram or creating user-generated content (UGC) the brand can post on their own page. If you have a high-quality camera, you could offer to take product photos or flatlays in exchange for comped items.

So how *do* you ask a brand to send you free stuff? We've met creators in the past who feel awkward and uncomfortable doing this. But keep in mind all of the work you've put into content creation and how normal it is for brands and companies to gift things to creators. You deserve some creator rewards for your efforts! Also, the brands getting free, earned media from your content is a bonus for them, making it a win-win for everyone! First things first: whether you're contacting a brand through email or a direct message (DM) on social media, it's critical that you make sure you are following their page before you contact them. Your message should be clear and concise. State what you want from the brand and, most importantly, explain what you plan to offer in return. We cannot stress this part enough! Don't be vague or obscure about how you plan to add value to the brand. Really spell this part out and make it crystal clear to the brand what they will be getting in return. This is especially important for smaller creators who have just a few thousand followers, as some brands only have limited products or experiences to give, and sometimes will just immediately reject smaller creators because they don't feel like they're getting enough return on investment (ROI). We hate saying that you need to prove yourself to a brand, but sometimes making it clear how you'll integrate their products can be the difference between a yes and a no.

One thing that many creators should focus on is making their messages more personal. Compliment the product. If you're messaging a cookie brand, for example, say how delicious the cookies look and maybe even name a specific flavor or two that caught your eye. (For examples of what brand outreach should look like, see chapter 12.)

There are numerous ways to make your offer stand out, and you can tailor it based on your level of enthusiasm for the product. This approach will always be more effective than blindly sending the same message to hundreds of brands. It is fine to reach out to multiple companies. Some will say yes, some will say no, some may agree and then disappear, and others may never reply at all. That is just part of the process. But how you approach them makes all the difference. A thoughtful and respectful message can lead to long-term partnerships, while a sloppy, generic one can end up being mocked or ignored.

The Cost of "Free" Stuff

There may be times when you don't want freebies. Maybe you already have the item being offered. Maybe it's something you just don't want or need. Perhaps the brand is asking for too much off the bat. Whatever the reason, there might be times when you simply don't want to accept a freebie, and that's okay! Rejecting things that don't suit you or don't fit organically in your content is entirely acceptable. Never feel obligated to go out of your way to promote something you don't want or don't need.

Brands that are too demanding

Sometimes the brand providing the product is way too demanding. Sometimes that "free" gift comes with too many strings, too many expectations, and way too much of your time.

Not long ago, a major movie studio sent us some PR boxes for a movie that was about to be released in theaters. The box included a bunch of goodies like a custom-themed robe, a candle, beauty products, and some cute kitchen utensils. Cool, right? We thought so, too, until someone from the studio called and texted Marissa on her personal phone, demanding to know why we didn't post about the freebies right away. We were stunned. The only reason they even had our phone numbers was because the shipping label required them.

To us, that crossed a serious line. Digging through delivery info to chase someone down over a free box? To us, this was a huge overstep, violating our privacy and crossing professional boundaries.

We were so annoyed, we drafted a few strongly worded email replies. One of them even included a photo of the growing tower of cardboard boxes piled inside the front door, along with a stern message letting them know they weren't the only brand waiting for an "urgent" post. In the end, we deleted our drafted emails and chose silence instead. This is the downside of accepting too many freebies. When you take anything and everything, not only can it create a physical amount of clutter in your space, but it's also stressful when companies get overly demanding.

Without a preexisting contract or arrangement, what are they going to do? Take back the experience? Deduct it from the nonexistent paycheck they're giving you? We did post about the box eventually, within a few days, which is a perfectly reasonable and standard amount of time to post about a freebie. It's not uncommon for influencers to take a month or even a few months. We did, however, make a mental note to not accept PR product boxes from that company again, as it was not worth the ask.

We also had a negative experience with a brand that gifted us some clothing. The clothes were fine, although not all of them fit. To fulfill our end of the bargain, we created a few Instagram stories that featured the clothing. But apparently, that wasn't enough for this brand. They then sent numerous messages demanding that we also create an IG reel. We politely, but firmly, refused.

The brand then had the audacity to send us an invoice of about $200 for the clothing we had received! They sent an email explaining that, because we didn't feature the clothing in a reel, we were required to pay them the retail cost of the clothing. We were shocked at their nerve! Our first reaction was anger and annoyance.

But then we calmly opened up our laptop and created an invoice of our own. We sent them a $600 invoice for the Instagram stories we created along with an email asking how they would like to make arrangements to pay us for our services. We didn't get a reply, but they also stopped bothering us about the cost of the clothes.

The difficult thing is that you often have no idea whether a brand will be chill or demanding until you start working with them. Don't be hard on yourself if you find yourself in that situation. Fortunately, there are ways to gauge how a brand treats creators before you get roped into a deal with them.

Identifying and responding to difficult brands

No one should have to deal with harassment, but unfortunately, sometimes brands do harass influencers.

Here are a few red flags to look out for when accepting free products from a brand:

- Use of extreme or hyperbolic language such as "urgent," "critical," or even "emergency"
- Demanding a very tight or completely unrealistic deadline

- Speaking down to you, belittling your work, or acting as if your time isn't valuable
- Trying to intimidate you, such as by threatening to sue you if you do not adhere to their demands

When it comes to these situations, we feel it's best to send one firm response addressing the issue, and then ignore all future communications from the brand. If they want additional posts, whitelisting/reupload rights, or anything extra like this, you can send them a rate for the suggested additional work. If they didn't like the content you posted, you can offer to delete it if it's a static post. If it's a story that's already expired, then you can, once again, offer a branded campaign with scripted content for next time. When you bring up your sponsored rates, brands trying to finesse additional posts will typically back off. You can even filter their messages into a folder if it upsets you to see them.

When those freebies are just clutter

Have you ever heard the expression "too much of a good thing"?

Another reason to say no to a freebie is if the brand is offering something you don't want or need. It can be hard to turn down free items, especially if they are expensive. It can be especially difficult to turn down free stuff if you grew up in a low-income household where you couldn't afford certain luxuries.

When we first started our influencer journey, the idea of getting free stuff in the mail every week (or sometimes every day!) would have sounded like a dream. We'd jump up and down over a free lipstick. Just imagine how thrilled we thought we'd be over thousands of dollars' worth of free beauty products.

But eventually, the sparkle wears off. Unboxing turns into a chore. Trash piles up. Your space starts feeling more like a storage unit. When your shelves are full, your closet is overflowing, and you're staring at three nearly identical face creams wondering how this became your life, you realize . . . too much of a good thing is still too much. If it feels like more work than it's worth, that's your cue to start saying no.

Melissa Tierney, the influencer we mentioned in earlier chapters, says, "You have to pick and choose your battles when it comes to free products and experiences versus getting paid. Disney Parks is not going to pay creators; they just won't. For example, I won't ask for money if I'm getting something like expensive diamonds. That's a value to me if you're sending me a diamond tennis bracelet for $2K."

The Perks of Being Compensated with Freebies

Although accepting freebies can present some challenges, there are perks! Freebies can be awesome in certain situations, especially if it's something you typically buy anyway or a unique experience that you couldn't re-create on your own. The financial ups and downs of being a full-time content creator are unpredictable, but the plus side is the constant opportunity for loads of comped goods and services that could easily add up to tens of thousands of dollars if you were to purchase them on your own. Unique experiences are in a league of their own, with many of them being things that money couldn't even buy, like accessing a closed-off portion of Disneyland or getting a behind-the-scenes look on a private movie set from a studio. Whatever it is, there are advantages to doing things the influencer way.

When the freebie is something you'd buy anyway

Who doesn't love free stuff? Freebies can be especially helpful for big life moments. For example, they can offset costs for special occasions or events like planning a wedding, moving into a new place, or having a baby. Anyone who has ever put together a baby registry or picked out furniture for an apartment knows how quickly those costs add up (better put out some home decor content so you can ask for free furniture! Just kidding . . . not).

A few years ago, Shanna got engaged and started planning her wedding. So, of course, she turned to YouTube for help with the planning process.

Many of those videos covered the terrifying topic of wedding budgets. That's when we learned that, in Southern California a $100,000 wedding budget was considered modest. When she began crunching the numbers, the over five-figure flower estimates, wedding planners, photographers, venues, music, and food became overwhelming. The feeling of dread and horror sunk in as she wondered how everything added up so quickly and was so expensive.

After a few weeks of being overwhelmed and paralyzed by sticker shock, she put on her influencer cap. We make content in the lifestyle space, and weddings count as lifestyle, don't they? You bet they do! So she started exploring ways to offset some of the wedding costs by partnering up with some wedding companies. Well, fast-forward a few months later, and "let's see if I can get some free wedding stuff" evolved into getting approximately $25K worth of wedding goods and services gifted to her in exchange for creating and posting content. Those "freebies" included an engagement photoshoot, two wedding dresses, a veil, shoes, hair and makeup services, invitations and signage, flowers, decor, uplighting, and wedding rings.

It wasn't "free" in the way people might think, because we worked for it, often very hard, creating high-quality content for brands. Most of the content took several hours setting up shots and editing video and photo content to each brand's specifications.

Rather than getting a paycheck that Shanna would have to spend on the wedding, she found a way to get the goods and services she needed to plan a beautiful wedding without spending her own money. That's a win in our book!

When you're comped unique experiences

When people think of freebies, they usually think of tangible products, but one type of freebie we absolutely love to pursue is in-person experiences. They don't take up space in your home or collect dust on a shelf, but rather offer something completely different.

Someone once said that travel is the only thing you buy that makes you richer. Experiences allow you to share special moments with friends and create lasting memories together.

While enjoying the free creator perks can start to feel normal after a while, noncreator guests and plus-ones still typically find the experience extra exciting and thrilling. Shanna's husband is not an influencer at all and never posts about himself online. Sometimes we get a little jaded or bored by all the free experiences we receive, but he is always amazed. When Shanna and her husband started dating, he jokingly called her "Barbie with dates included" because she always took him on fun, no-cost dates by providing tickets to plays, restaurant openings, movie screenings, and more.

Here are examples of experiences you could be gifted in exchange for promotional content:

- **Travel expenses** (like cruises, plane tickets, and hotel stays)
- **Tickets to performances** (like movies, plays, and concerts)
- **Tickets to sports games**
- **Exercise classes or personal training**
- **Beauty treatments** (like massages, facials, haircuts, and styling)
- **Plastic surgery and procedures** (such as Botox, acupuncture, laser treatments, fat freezing, and more. Influencers have even been comped nose and boob jobs as well.)
- **Admission to theme or water parks**
- **Meals at restaurants**
- **Art classes**
- **Photography sessions**

These experiences provide you with the opportunity to get out and explore, spend quality time with friends or family, and, of course, inspiration for new content. Influencers may even get special treatment, like being upgraded to VIP, great seats, or preferred parking. We love being compensated with unique experiences because these are the kinds of things we would usually create content about or pay for anyway. These experiences are often visually interesting and make for beautiful, engaging content. Plus, it is fun to have a social calendar filled with exciting events.

Overall, navigating freebies can be tricky terrain. The best things to remember are to remain professional at all times, keep the line of communication open, and stand your ground when a brand tries to take advantage of you. Freebies are not all you should be striving for, but they certainly are a delightful perk of the job.

14

The Scoop on Contracts

The very first brand deal we ever did was with a popular nail polish brand sold at drugstores across the country. We were beyond excited and quickly e-signed the contract while skimming it over for around thirty seconds. This deal was for a thousand dollars! To a newbie creator, a four-figure deal was nothing to snub your nose at! We were thrilled with that amount. Almost immediately, we started planning what we would do with the money.

We dragged our butts to the beach and filmed a cute video at the Santa Monica pier, making sure the Los Angeles landmark featured prominently in the background. We each planned multiple outfit changes and did close-ups of the product. We even filmed ourselves splashing and frolicking in the ice-cold waves. We worked our butts off filming that video.

Then we got home and worked our butts off some more editing it. We carefully spliced together camera shots, agonized over the best takes to use, and chose background music. Finally, we had a finished video in hand (well, on our computers, but you know what we mean!).

We proudly submitted it to the brand, confident that they would be blown away. Maybe the brand would love the video so much that they would hire us for a national campaign in CVS? Why not dream big?

A few days later, we received an email that crushed all those grand dreams. With one curt, impersonal sentence, we were informed that the brand was canceling the campaign. Our carefully crafted video, meticulously filmed and edited over several days, would never see the light of day.

Okay, so they're canceling the video, but at least they would still pay us the thousand dollars for all the work we did, right? *Right?* After all our hard work and effort, the brand was only going to pay us . . . a measly one hundred dollars?! That couldn't be right.

Finally, we did what we should have done from the beginning. We read the contract. It was about ten pages long, filled with boring fine print, but we sat down and read every word. There it was, on page five, under the section labeled "Cancellation."

"In the event of a cancellation, talent shall receive 10 percent of the overall fee." Ten percent of a thousand dollars was, indeed, a hundred bucks.

We were shocked, devastated, and angry. We felt betrayed and taken advantage of. For years afterward, we both refused to buy or wear that brand of nail polish because we didn't want to support the company that had done us dirty.

But we'll tell you this much—we never let it happen again. From that point forward, we always made sure we were aware of the terms we were agreeing to and understood the consequences of those terms. And in every contract we signed from then on, we asked to be paid 100 percent of our fee in the event of cancellation.

That nail polish debacle, though painful, left us smarter, savvier, and a whole lot less naïve. Oh yeah, and we ended up cutting out the brand's portion of the video, editing out every single brand logo, and posting it on YouTube anyway as a cute summer fashion video. It performed well for us and was a good way to turn lemons into lemonade since we now had a surplus of fun B-roll beach footage. (Unless explicitly stated in an agreement, you can sometimes repurpose some of the content from a canceled deal.)

This chapter is all about the ins and outs of contracts in the influencer space. We explain some of the essentials of what to look out for when accepting a deal and signing an agreement.

We've been through it all! We've filmed the most comprehensive and elaborate videos for brands, as well as the most basic sit-and-talk videos similar to those QVC ads where they describe and sell you an item. Being prepped on what to expect in a creator legal agreement and wisely negotiating could be the difference between ending up with 10 percent (or even 0 percent) of your paycheck after doing all the work, or 100 percent.

Every single brand is different and every brand has a different contract. Some brands, typically smaller, more informal ones, might tell you they don't want to use a contract, that it's unnecessary. We believe that any time money is exchanged, there should always be a contract, even if the brand doesn't want one. It's good for both parties, as it holds both parties accountable. If you don't have a contract, there is always the risk that they will have you do all the work, and then they won't pay you. Even when you do have a contract, you're still taking on that risk, but with no contract, the risk is even greater.

The Anatomy of a Contract

Contracts can feel intimidating and scary when you don't understand what you're signing. Let's dissect all the parts of the contract so you know what to look for the next time you enter a contracted deal. And if you don't understand or it isn't clearly specified, you should email and ask for written clarification.

Cancellations

Remember our nail polish story? Trust us, you do not want that to happen to you! If you put in the time and effort of making the content, you want to make sure you get paid.

One thing we require in every one of our contracts is "Pay or Play." This is the line we always ask to put in our contracts:

"Pay or Play. If the campaign is canceled due to no breach of agreement by Influencer, and Influencer has rendered services, then Influencer is to receive full fee for production of content."

You want to make sure that if the brand cancels on you, through no fault of your own, that you receive the full amount of money. Don't be afraid to require this kind of language in your own contracts! It's not as big of an ask as you might think. Nearly all the brands we've worked with since the nail polish ordeal have agreed to pay us the full amount in the event of a cancellation. However, there have been a handful of brands who could not agree to that. Sometimes it was because we were doing the deal through an agency and they couldn't guarantee when the brand would pay. In those cases, use the information you have available to decide if you want to take that risk. Does the brand or agency seem credible or sketchy? Have you worked with them before? Do you know of any other creators who've worked with them and had a positive or negative experience? It's good to know what you're getting into.

Payment details

When will the brand pay you? Will you get paid up front or after the campaign goes live? Every deal is different. We find it common in this industry to get paid "Net 30." This simply means thirty days after the content goes live, but sometimes it means thirty days after they receive the invoice.

Some deals will pay you the entire amount up front upon signing the contract. Some deals will pay you half upon signing the contract, and half when you send them the video draft. We love doing those kinds of deals because we're getting paid the entire amount before the content even goes live, minimizing the risk that the brand will cancel the campaign or go AWOL. Some deals will pay you half upon delivering the content, and half after it goes live.

Will you get paid through PayPal? Direct deposit? Is it a foreign payment? If so, the brand may ask for additional payment information, like a SWIFT code and International Bank Account Number (IBAN). Keep in mind, however, that many brands will not always hunt you down for your banking details. It's up to you, the creator, to provide the brand with all the information they need to pay you properly. Doing so reduces the chances of delays. We even had a separate calendar at one point just to mark down the dates and deadlines related to brand deals and payments. This turned out to be super helpful because it presented all the complex details in a clear visual.

Transaction fees

Beware of transaction fees! We recommend including a line in the contract that states that the fees are the responsibility of the brand. Trust us! That way, later on, when they send you only $950 of your $1,000 payment and say it's because fees were removed, you can refer to a section of the contract stating that it's their responsibility to pay those fees. This line can simply say, "Fees to be covered by vendor."

If the payment is being processed via wire transfer, the fees will typically range from $15 to $40, but again, this could vary. Direct deposit generally is a better option because there isn't a fee. PayPal fees are exorbitant, so we suggest brands include extra funds to cover them if they choose to use this payment method.

Invoices

Creating an invoice may seem daunting, but there are tons of free templates online. Typically, they all include a few standard details:

- The date the invoice is submitted
- A short description of the project
- The amount of money owed (with the appropriate currency specified)
- Your legal name and address
- The brand's name and address
- Your payment information (account number, routing number, bank name, and so on)

You'll want to promptly send your invoice after submitting your work or when the content goes live. And by "promptly," we mean you better send it immediately (or as soon as you remember!) because that's usually when the "Net 30" clock starts ticking. If you wait a week to send your invoice, then your payment is going to be delayed by an additional week, and that's on you! We have had payments delayed by weeks because we forgot to send an invoice, so don't make the same mistake we did.

The brand may request more information after you send them your invoice. For example, some brands will want an invoice number.

As mentioned earlier, international brands often ask for extra financial details, such as a SWIFT code and IBAN.

Content creation deadlines

You, as the content creator, should do things by the book. You don't want to give the brand any reason to have problems with you. We find that clear communication works best when dealing with brands. They are used to influencers being flaky, so instead, surprise them by being overly professional. To that end, we like to include a clear timeline in our contracts.

Whitelisting

Often, brands will request whitelisting or pre-roll ad rights in your contracts. This means that they want to take your content and use it in a paid ad, for which you need to request money. This money needs to be discussed and agreed on up front, not just snuck into the contract. We recommend that when you first quote a brand you include a little section in your rate card for a whitelisting/pre-roll fee. Even if it's something modest like a few hundred dollars or less depending on your size. This way, if a brand tries to sneak it in the contract later, you can refer back to your original quote. If you're creating content for your own audience, that's one thing, but the brand needs to pay you if they want to use your content in a paid advertisement.

Typically, licensing usage rights are decided depending on the length of time the brand intends to use your content. Some influencers request a monthly fee; others offer rights for six months or one year. Sometimes a brand will pay to use your content in perpetuity, which means forever. It's up to you what you charge for this and how you choose to structure the deal. First, you and the brand should come to an understanding about what the brand wants to do with your content. Then you can discuss the fees and the length of the license.

What If the Brand Refuses to Pay?

A contract can offer some protection and leverage, but it is not foolproof, which is a tough lesson to learn. People break contracts shockingly often.

It can feel absolutely enraging when a brand doesn't pay you what or when you were expecting. It's a total lack of respect for your time, effort, and professionalism. It can make you feel so small and powerless. If you're lucky, this is a problem you will never have to encounter. We certainly hope that every brand you work with is professional and pays you on time and there are no problems. But if a brand ever fails to pay you, there are steps to take to move things along.

Send a friendly reminder

First, send the brand a professional email reminding them that they still need to pay you. Your email should be factual, brief, and straightforward. Try to keep the emotion out of it!

Here is an example. We sent this email to a spray tanning company that tried to cancel the campaign and pay us in free product.

> Our payment is now 15 days past due. We kindly ask you to release our $3500 USD payment as soon as possible. Thank you for your attention to this matter.
>
> Best,
>
> Shanna Lisa & Marissa Rachel

Hopefully, the brand will respond, agree that they owe you the money, and pay it promptly. If the brand doesn't respond, or responds but gives you the runaround ("Check is in the mail! Sorry, it's a holiday! Sorry, our payments person is on maternity leave!"), then it's time to send a legal letter.

Pull out the big guns with a legal letter

This is an unfortunate but often necessary step to take when dealing with someone who doesn't want to pay you. A legal letter is used to communicate, inform, advise, demand action, and confirm agreements. In this case, it's typically meant to nudge a brand into paying you when other email efforts have been unsuccessful.

Most people are intimidated at the thought of hiring a lawyer because they assume it will be ridiculously expensive. But you don't need to hire a lawyer to draft the letter for you. You could save money by writing out the initial letter yourself, then contacting a lawyer to have them review it, sign it, and email it to the brand on your behalf. Most lawyers will perform this service for a reasonable price.

We've had to send legal letters to several brands, and the letters have almost always motivated the brand to pay us. So, it can be worth it to contact a lawyer and have them send a letter. It often lets brands know that you're serious and not willing to let them get away with cheating you out of your payment.

Here's an example:

Email subject line: PAST DUE unpaid payment due for services in the amount of $5,000

Lawyer's Name

Attorney at Law

123 Address Street
Your City, Your State

Email: lawyersemail@gmail.com
(555) 555-5555

Today's Date

Name of person you've been communicating with

Add any other names here, such as people who work in finance or legal department

Brand Name

Brand Address

Re: Marissa Rachel

Amount Due: $5,000.00 USD and statutory penalties

Dear Ms. *Brand Employee*,

This Office represents Marissa Rachel, in connection with certain services performed by Marissa Rachel for you, and each of you, and Brand Name. On December 7, 2024, she was presented with an offer of $5,000.00 USD in exchange for services to be rendered. Marissa Rachel began performing services from December 7, 2024, to December 26, 2024, but despite requests, the full payment was not paid or otherwise tendered by you. The total of $5,000.00 USD remains unpaid and past due.

Ms. Rachel is not willing to discount the amount as the proper and full amount is due and owing. The past due balance owed is $5,000.00 USD. Pursuant to California Civil Code section 1717.5 et al. statutory penalties and legal fees for

> the unpaid amount may be recoverable. The State of California and the US Department of Labor also have authority to assess penalties due to unpaid wages in its investigation.
>
> Please contact this Office immediately to make arrangements for the payment of the sums due. If we do not hear from you within 14 days from the date hereof, we will have no alternative but to pursue all lawful means for this matter. Ms. Rachel looks forward to future amicable relations pending this resolution.
>
> Sincerely,
> *Lawyer's Name*
> *Attorney at Law*

Notice how we include basic information, such as when services were rendered and when the agreement was entered into? There is sometimes a stigma that creators are unprofessional, and this legal letter brings the correct tone when asking for an overdue payment from a brand. If you can, we recommend including the lawyer's contact information so that the brand can contact the attorney directly.

Important Takeaways

The truth about contracts is that they are often a necessary evil. Whether you're just starting out or have a full team supporting you, taking even thirty minutes to read through a contract before signing can make a huge difference in your long-term success.

Knowing the details, especially the worst-case scenarios, helps you stay prepared for things that might be out of your control. It's much better than being caught off guard if a brand suddenly cancels or delays payment for months. We've seen both of those situations in contracts before, and we've had to push back on clauses that would have left us unprotected.

When you understand your rights as a creator, you're in a much better position to stay calm and think clearly when problems come up. It allows you to work with the brand on a fair solution instead of reacting from a place of stress or panic. That mindset not only helps you navigate tough situations, but it also strengthens your reputation and your brand in the long run.

Contracts are a crucial part of this business, but they can often feel overwhelming. As a result, many creators don't take contracts as seriously as they should. And unfortunately, a slight shift in phrasing can cost you a ton of money and create a lot of stress. That's why we want to leave you with some brief but super important advice regarding contracts.

Read every word of your contract yourself

It's amazing how many people don't do this. Especially important if you're signing a contract with a brand you've never worked with before, reading contracts is still necessary even if you have a good relationship with them.

If you have an agent or manager who has promised to read all your contracts, read it yourself anyway. We have caught mistakes in contracts many times, even with trusted representatives supposedly reviewing them! Eventually, you'll get to the point where it'll become like second nature, and you'll be able to easily decipher contracts yourself with confidence. Practice makes perfect!

Don't be afraid to ask for changes

This is incredibly important. Many new creators feel intimidated by contracts and mistakenly believe they need to accept everything the brand offers. But the contract the brand presents is a suggested draft, not a finalized set of rules you are required to follow.

Redlines are a very normal part of negotiations. You should feel empowered to ask for changes that benefit you and your business, whether that's getting your payment faster, specifying that transaction fees should be the brand's responsibility, or removing sneaky language that holds you to ridiculous or unfair expectations.

15

Working with Agents and Managers

A manager once told us, "You'll *never, ever* work with a car company." The next year we booked a campaign with Toyota SoCal for the LA Auto Show. The same manager told us that no agent would want to represent us. Within a year, we were signed with one of the largest agencies in Los Angeles, where we would often run into different celebrities in the lobby, like Will Ferrell and Patrick Dempsey.

Managers and agents are hit or miss—let's just get that out of the way. They can be amazing, and undoubtedly some of them can do incredible things for your career. However, some can be a nightmare. Picking the right agent and manager can unlock doors that would take you years to break through on your own. But choosing or sticking with the wrong people can have terrible repercussions on your career and limit your opportunities. So, it's important to know what to look for when choosing representation. You may even decide that working with agents and managers isn't for you!

The Differences Between Agents and Managers

Let's explore some key differences between these two different types of representatives. Knowing everything may help you make a more informed decision should you go that route in the future. It may be beneficial to wait to explore hiring an agent or manager until your content gains more traction. Or maybe you want to hire someone right away. There are different ways to go about it. But it's better to prepare you on what to expect beforehand than for you to get one and decide later that it's not what you thought it would be. We've personally had a mixed experience with representatives, so we're here to guide you through the process.

What they do

An agent is a legally licensed representative who submits you for work, secures jobs for you, and negotiates contracts on your behalf. Some of the largest and most well-known entertainment talent agencies, known as the "Big Three," include Creative Artists Agency (CAA), William Morris Endeavor (WME), and United Talent Agency (UTA).

A manager's job focuses more on your long-term career path and the day-to-day operations of your business. They provide career advice, business management, and shape the overall direction in which your career should go. They typically have a smaller list of clients with whom they maintain a more personal relationship.

While agents are licensed by the state, managers are not licensed. In simple language, that means anyone, anywhere, can wake up one day and decide to call themselves a manager.

How much they take

Agents are not allowed to commission more than 10 percent of their client's earnings.

There are no limits on the percentage a manager can commission. In the influencer space, we have seen managers charge as low as 10 percent commission and as high as 60 percent commission. In our experience, 20 percent seems to be the average.

When You Should Consider Representation

Some influencers have both an agent and a manager. Others have either a manager or an agent, but not both. And many choose to forgo representation and run the show themselves.

> Some content creators, particularly top-performing influencers, hire their own in-house manager who works for only them. While a traditional manager could have their attention divided among twenty or so clients on their roster, the advantage of an in-house manager is that they spend all their time working for one person—you. The clear disadvantage of this approach is that while most managers work on commission, an in-house manager requires a set salary that you're on the hook for, whether they book you any gigs or not.

There is definitely no "one size fits all" approach with management. Every creator has different needs. Typically, there are two scenarios where getting a manager or agent may be beneficial and add value to your business and brand: if you're a rookie looking for support, or if your business is growing exponentially and you need help managing the workload.

Starting out as a rookie

When you first start out as a content creator, chances are you probably won't be booking an excessive number of deals right out of the gate. There can be some cool, unpaid opportunities that can absolutely benefit smaller creators, like attending fun movie premieres, parties, brand events, and brand trips or getting included on gifting PR lists. So for those reasons alone, you may want to consider representation as a newer creator trying to get yourself out there and make the most of your experience and creator journey. However, a con might be that they will sign you as a tactic in case you blow up and not offer much in the way of monetary value.

Struggling to balance the workload

As a content creator, you have to manage a ton of behind-the-scenes work most people don't see. You must come up with unique, fresh ideas for shoots, and sometimes script them beforehand. Then there's the actual execution of shooting that content, editing it, as well as all the effects that go hand in hand with posting, such as closed captioning, titles, thumbnails or covers, lighting, sound quality, music, voiceovers, tags, descriptions, collaborators, and so on. All of this is super time-consuming!

While making all this content, adding brand outreach and networking to earn more money can be overwhelming. The business portion of earning a living on social media can feel like you're running on a hamster wheel of doom, always chasing the next deal and opportunity. The struggle is real!

This is where it can be beneficial to seek out representation. If you feel like you're unable to keep up with the demand, or if posting content and pursuing sponsored opportunities and partnerships feels unattainable or unmanageable with the time you have, then it might be time to consider representation. That way, an agent can manage your paid opportunities, and a manager can take care of events and the long-term strategy for your digital career.

When You Shouldn't Consider Representation

Considering representation is not always a good idea. For some creators, it's a wise redirection of time, effort, and energy. But then there are the creators who hire representation just because they are lazy. They think hiring an agent or manager will magically make their follower and view count skyrocket. (It doesn't.)

Discerning if you just *want* a manager to make life easier versus if you *need* a manager because your business has reached a certain level where it makes sense to have one can be a struggle. Don't let the perceived prestige and glamour of the idea of being important enough to have a manager cloud your judgment on whether it's really a necessity.

Content creator Melissa Tierney says, "You're your own best advocate. What I recommend is building a team and having assistants or support instead of hiring an agent who's just trying to get a commission and negotiate deals. Sometimes agents will not present opportunities if they feel the rate is too low or if they just don't like the brand."

You shouldn't bring on a manager or agent just because you want a "hands-off" experience. Social media is a hands-on career, and you still need to read your contracts, stay aware of your brand relationships, and steer your business. Some creators look for a "magic fix," but representation doesn't guarantee success. It's simply a way to delegate certain business tasks and take a bit off your plate, not a shortcut to growth.

Connecting with Agents and Managers

There are generally two ways to secure representation. Either a manager reaches out to you, or you take the initiative and approach them. If you are the one making the first move, it helps to be strategic with your pitch. A strong way to position yourself is to highlight how your content and personal brand align with the creators they already represent. This shows that you would be a natural addition to their roster and that your work fits into the kinds of partnerships they are already securing for their talent. Framing yourself as a good match makes it easier for them to see the value in working with you.

How do you find an influencer manager? One great place to start is to look at creators who are similar to you (meaning same genre of content) and see who their managers are. Sometimes their email address in their bio can yield clues. Other times, you may be able to find their manager through a Google search. You can also figure it out based on who they're following or who they post. On occasion, you can also find it through their Internet Movie Database (IMDb) page, if they have one.

Find the manager's contact email on their company's website, their Instagram or TikTok bio, or their LinkedIn page. Take some time to study their experience and history working with influencers. Does it seem like they've just started? Or are they well-established and have been doing this a while? Do they have any press written about them? Look at the creators they represent. Do those creators look like they're doing a lot of paid work? Do they rarely post any sponsorships or do they post sponsorships all the time? Are the brands similar to ones you want to be working with? Are they well-known, big-name brands, or brands you've never heard of? What other opportunities do their clients seem to be doing?

If you like what you see, and want to reach out, go ahead and send them an email.

Drafting your outreach

Keep it short and concise. Brag about yourself as much as possible. Your main goal of your email should be to get them interested and intrigued enough that they meet with you, either over a phone call, a video call, or in person.

Your email should follow this basic format:

> [Friendly Greeting]
>
> [One to two sentences to introduce yourself.]
>
> [State the most impressive fact about your social media career. We like to put the most compelling fact right at the beginning of the email where they're most likely to see it. Really spend some time to think about which impressive fact about yourself you want to share. Don't just assume after five minutes of thinking that you don't have anything impressive enough to share. Maybe it's a big follower number or view number, maybe it's how fast your account has been growing, maybe it's a piece of news media you were featured in, or maybe it's a noteworthy collab you did.]
>
> [Describe your content more in depth, and list any other noteworthy career-related achievements.]
>
> [Tell them why you're contacting them. You're seeking representation and would love to speak with them.]
>
> [Add a sign-off, as well as a reminder of how best to contact you.]

Overall, keep your message captivating, professional, and brief. Here's an example of the email we sent, which got us meetings with all the top agencies in LA. It's very, very specific to our unique situation and isn't replicable, but the point is to show you the structure.

> Subject line: TV Host & YouTuber with 1.5 Million Subs Seeking Representation
>
> Hi!
>
> My name is Marissa and I run the Marissa Rachel YouTube channel. I currently have 1.5+ million subscribers and am continuing to grow—I've gained approximately 1 million subscribers in the last year. I typically get between 5 and 10 million video views per month.
>
> My channel is a "lifestyle" channel geared toward an audience of young women. In the past, I've had success working with brands in beauty, fashion, fitness, and women's health-related products.
>
> I've hosted four seasons of *Ready, Set, Style*, a reality fashion show produced by AwesomenessTV and distributed by Verizon's go90. It also airs on television in the UK on the ITV2 network.
>
> I'm currently seeking representation, and I'd love to speak with you! I'm located in Los Angeles, so an in-person meeting would also be possible.
>
> Thank you so much! Looking forward to hearing from you! :)
> —Marissa
>
> [links to all of your social media accounts]

Questions to consider when hiring a representative

At some point during the hiring process, you'll talk to the agent or manager over the phone, via video chat, or in person. Make sure you are prepared for that meeting! The fact is that some managers and agents tend to oversell, overpromise, and exaggerate elements that they can bring to the table, but asking the right questions can help you decipher what working with that person will be like and if they are a good fit for you.

When choosing and signing with a manager, move with caution, read the contracts carefully before signing, and make sure that you know exactly what you're getting into.

Keep these questions in mind when speaking with a potential representative:

- What percentage of your income will they commission? Is this amount consistent with that of other managers and agents in this space, or is it wildly different than the average? (For example, a manager asking for 70 percent of your income would be considered extremely high.)
- Is the commission the same whether the deal is an inbound offer (meaning a brand reached out to me with an offer) or if the rep sought it out? In our experience, some reps charge a flat-rate commission across the board, whereas others charge less if the deal landed in their inbox without them having to work for it.
- Will they commission all of your income or only a certain part of it? (For example, someone who is a model/actress/influencer may assume the representative will only be commissioning their influencer activities, whereas the rep may intend on commissioning all their entertainment jobs.)

- Will you be required to put their email address in your bio? Or will you merely be forwarding them the emails that require their assistance? Will you still have access to your own emails from brands? Will you be CC'd or BCC'd on negotiation emails?
- How many other clients do they represent? Will they be spread too thin and unable to give you enough personal attention?
- Are their other clients similar to you or different? (There's an argument both ways. Generally speaking, reps tend to specialize in a particular niche. Maybe it's mommy bloggers, maybe it's gamers, maybe it's comedians. But on the flip side, some managers seek a more diverse stable of talent.)
- Who will be your main point of contact? Is the person you are speaking with going to be your main point of contact? (In our experience, it's actually very common that the person you speak to during the onboarding interview may not be your direct point of contact. It's common to pass you off to an assistant for day-to-day activities.) Is this person a hiring manager who will later match you up with a manager?
- What happens if you don't connect with the person assigned to you? Can you ask to work with someone different?
- How often do you expect to meet with them? Will you have a weekly check-in call whether there is a deal on the table or not? Will you have a monthly lunch meeting? Or will you only meet sporadically once every few months? Will your schedules be aligned?
- How far do they live from you? Are in-person meetings even a possibility or will all your communication be virtual?
- What connections do they have in your industry space? Do they have connections to brands, TV or film producers, photographers, media outlet editors, publicists, and so on?

- Are you both in alignment about the direction of your career? Do they want you to change your content, your appearance, or your target audience? Are there any areas they see room for improvement? How do they think you can make yourself more attractive and marketable to reach the opportunities you are seeking? Do you share the same goals in terms of where you see your career headed over the next five years?
- Does this person speak intelligently? Do they write coherent, professional emails, or are their messages full of typos and errors? This is important because this person is going to be representing you and will be communicating on your behalf in writing. You want their communications to reflect positively on you.
- How long do they want you to commit to signing? Generally, shorter contracts favor the influencer because they give you more flexibility, especially if this is someone you've just met and never worked with before. In our opinion, if they want you to sign a contract longer than one year, that's too long and you should push back and ask for one year.
- Are they willing to commit to a trial period? Perhaps three to six months to try things out and see how you like working together before signing a longer contract?
- If you decide to end your professional working relationship, how do you do so? Do they require one month's notice? Six months' notice?
- Do you like this person's overall vibe and communication style? Did you click? Will you feel comfortable reaching out and asking them questions, or do they seem unapproachable?

Red Flags to Look Out for When Working with Representatives

Here are a few things to look out for when working with a representative!

The rep ghosts you

Industry professionals can be very unresponsive to emails and require a lot of follow-ups. We recently spoke with a manager who would often take two or more weeks to respond and required multiple follow-up emails. We'd plan on a day to speak, and then it would come and go with no response or reply. This is a pretty significant red flag if representation cannot even schedule an initial call or meeting without it feeling like a huge chore.

What if the person the rep fails to reply to is your dream brand? If your rep "forgets to respond," "misses the email," or claims that "the email went into their spam folder," then you, the creator, miss out on an amazing opportunity! You may consider that to be a hyperbolic example, but these are the kinds of scenarios you need to think about.

The rep constantly criticizes you

The "it's all your fault" rep is also one we've dealt with firsthand on a number of occasions. Reps will occasionally invent reasons why they are unable to make any progress on the business and branding side of things. They place the blame entirely on the creator and absolve themselves of responsibility. They might say something along the lines of "Well, unfortunately, we cannot do anything for you because of these decisions you made."

Criticizing someone's content is often an easy excuse managers use when they don't want to follow through on something. It's kind of like when someone breaks up with you and gives you a list of reasons. Some of them might be valid, but there's usually more they are not saying out loud. The "it's all your fault" type of rep overhypes what they bring to the table. Sometimes they'll talk a lot about nonmonetary opportunities they brought to the table, such as the events they got you into, the advice they gave you about your content, or the PR packages they helped you score.

The rep overhypes what they will do for you

We once had a manager who would not stop gushing about getting one of their other clients a free beauty subscription box from a brand we'll call FoxyBox. She must have said, "I got my client *six months* of FoxyBox for free" at least ten times. Out of curiosity, we looked up the value of the box and saw that two boxes retailed for around a hundred dollars total. She brushed it off when we told her that we had actually worked with FoxyBox before on multiple paid deals worth between five and ten thousand dollars each. So, sure, a free box is nice, but compared to what we had already done with the brand, it was not exactly the kind of win we'd shout from the rooftops. This behavior is a red flag in our book because it's overvaluing her abilities. This manager would also criticize paid campaigns, when the reality is that most creators would much prefer thousands of dollars for a paid deal as opposed to a $50 mystery box of products.

The rep only works with superstars

Some managers will only work with creators who have already made it big—meaning their representation comes with specific income requirements. The amount will vary: for some it's $100K+ a year; others will require $150K to $200K+ in inbound work. This is the quickest way to tell you that someone is a lower effort manager. Some managers will also brag about responding to emails and negotiating deals, but this is literally the bare minimum that a manager can do. These types of managers will gush about how they can get you the best deals ever and get you double or even triple the rate you ever could've gotten for yourself because of their magical persuasion skills. Usually, when we see a manager emphasize this again and again, it's because they're unable or unwilling to do the daunting task of getting paid work for you.

This kind of behavior tells you that they aren't looking to do much of the heavy lifting when it comes to securing brand deals. They expect the majority of that stuff to already come from you. If you are a creator who gets hit up often, with legitimate, non-spam offers and emails, then maybe this type of rep can work for you. However, this is not the case for most creators. Keep in mind that the main reason a manager might have these expectations of you, even going so far as to request tax returns up front, is because they want to be sure they'll earn a significant commission.

If you've been in this space for several years and earned around $200,000, then it will be relatively easy to figure out that the agent's 20 percent commission will be a nearly guaranteed $40,000 they are taking. However, if you were to flip the tables and ask how many dollars in deals they can guarantee for you, they will most likely have some convoluted answer alluding to the fact that they will simply not guarantee such a thing. Regardless, we'd recommend trying to do a trial run with this manager to determine if they are a good fit.

Green Flags That the Rep Is a Good Fit

While there can certainly be downsides to seeking representation, there can be overwhelming benefits to joining forces with the right rep. Below we list some beneficial qualities to look for in a manager or agent.

The rep is aligned with your goals

Something to always look for in representation is someone aligned with your overall goal and vision. Creators are not a one-size-fits-all species in terms of what we view as success. Creators can define success in the digital realm completely differently. Some might cite things like how much money you earn, the events and parties you attend, the number of views and likes on your content, or even how many fans approach you in the street. It's important to be on the same page as your representative and have an alignment of goals. You can determine a rep's plans for you by asking well-thought-out questions during your meetings with them. Get a sense of what they actively plan to do for you and the vision that they see for your social media journey. After all, they are, to a degree, an extension of your brand and business.

The rep is willing to do a trial period

This is a rare but promising opportunity. When a rep is willing to do a test run, it shows that they're invested in making this a mutually beneficial partnership and aren't simply trying to lock you into an agreement that doesn't serve you.

Most contracts that managers and agents will ask you to sign tend to, well, favor the managers or agents. They typically have no guarantees in them and commission all of your deals regardless of whether they secured it or not. Nearly all of the management we've met with have not been willing to do a trial run because they want their guaranteed money. However, if you are someone independently booking a lot of deals, you may want to insist on doing a trial period before you make a commitment.

You can work with the rep to determine the length of the trial period. For example, we've done three- to six-month trial periods, which is an optimal amount of time so you can see if the rep's efforts add value. One manager we met with over a nice Beverly Hills Hotel lunch felt very promising. We met, talked, laughed, shared some fries and lemonades, and discussed our goals in the digital space. At the end of the meal, she pulled a contract out of her purse, which asked us to sign away 20 percent of all of our future revenue to her. Despite enjoying our thirty-minute lunch meeting with her, we weren't convinced that we should give away that much of our business, which, at that point, we'd spent nearly a decade building up.

We proposed a trial period, and she immediately shot down the suggestion. If she'd agreed to even a month-long trial, things could have been very different. We aren't opposed to giving someone their commission, even one higher than 20 percent! It just has to be to the right person who demonstrates that they will benefit our business.

The rep is on top of things

Managers and agents are people, too, regular humans with everyday lives. They get busy with family, other clients, and life in general. That's normal. After all, their entire lives do not revolve around your success and career, but in business, it's important to be organized and responsive. A manager who is ordinarily quick to respond and doesn't need numerous follow-ups is a blessing. If they respond to 80 to 90 percent of your messages within twenty-four hours or so, then that's a pretty decent indicator they will be on top of things when communicating with brands on your behalf.

The rep is transparent without placing blame

We once had a manager look us in the eye at a coffee meeting and tell us our quality wasn't the best and could definitely use some improvement.

She didn't say it in a nasty or malicious way, but as an honest third party observing from the outside.

At the time, we were using a fairly cheap DSLR camera along with the webcam on a MacBook. After a short amount of self-reflection and deliberation, we realized that the manager was right. We could, and did, improve our quality. We invested in a nicer camera and saw amazing results. It's important that your agent/manager doesn't just tell you everything you want to hear but provides honest feedback, including what content is working well for you or what brands would like to see more of. You don't want a negative or critical rep, but being candid can help you pivot in the right direction when needed.

The rep takes accountability

Mistakes happen, but how a person handles the error is often more important than the mistake itself.

In one instance, we worked with a manager who accidentally missed an invoice we'd sent. We'd completed a deal with a manager and sent her the invoice shortly after completion. It was for a few thousand dollars, by no means our highest deal. We noticed a few weeks had gone by and our account still didn't have the money in it. By this time, the video had been posted for quite a while and had racked up a decent number of views. So we contacted the manager who was very apologetic. She said she would double check with her accounting employee to see what had happened and where the money was. This was fairly normal since nearly all agents and managers collect funds first, and then remove their cut and pay you your fee.

A few days later, we received a random and somewhat ominous-sounding text from her requesting a call from us. We immediately became nervous and ran through ideas of what had happened. *Maybe the brand didn't like the video and was refusing to pay us? What if they didn't feel like it got enough views or had sold enough of the product? What if they'd gone AWOL and just refused to pay us what was owed? Maybe they wanted a free make-good video (where brands have you create a second additional video at no extra charge because the first one didn't do well enough)?* We finally decided to muster up the courage and call her to see what was up.

"Guys!" she said, "I messed up and I'm so sorry about it!" She went on to explain how she was out of town when we'd sent the email and just missed it and never sent the invoice to her accountant until we'd followed up. She was having the accountant wire the money ASAP and we should have it within the next week. We could feel the fear and anxiety dissipate from our worried faces. "It's okay, no worries at all. We just wanted to make sure everything was okay and the money was still on its way!" we reassured her. The next week, just like the manager had promised, the money hit our account, and all was well. We often think about this manager and how she handled the situation with class and respect. She calmly acknowledged a mistake she made and fixed it. That level of professionalism speaks volumes.

When They Don't Want to Sign You

Not every agent or manager is going to be champing at the bit to sign you. There could be a multitude of different reasons for this. It might be that they feel like you aren't earning enough money or getting a lot of opportunities on your own, which is usually the case.

Most of the time, when they say no, they'll give a pretty standard response. Something along the lines of "being overwhelmed with too many clients and not having room to take on anyone new." And honestly, that might be true. Maybe they really are stretched thin with a bunch of other clients to attend to. Maybe they don't think you're a good fit for them.

Whatever the case, try not to take it personally. They have their reasons, but you have your own goals and a career you're trying to build. And you can absolutely do that with or without their help. A rejection is not the end of the road but a redirection. Besides, you don't want a mediocre manager signing you only to give you a subpar experience and possibly damage your overall brand.

Protecting Yourself from Scammers and Thieves

Not every person in this industry is who they seem. It is easy to assume that someone who acts friendly and seems helpful is trustworthy, but that is not always the case.

Marissa once worked at a company called StyleHaul, which was one of the first major YouTube networks. It represented many top creators, and she worked in the Hollywood office while also being a signed creator. During that time, one of her coworkers was Dennis Blieden. He held a key position in finance and was well-liked by many of the young women in the office. He always seemed polite, attentive, and good at solving problems. Although he wasn't an agent or manager himself, he held a senior role at a company that represented thousands of influencers. StyleHaul's entire model was built around managing creators, overseeing their payments, and securing brand deals on their behalf.

Dennis had access to the company's financial processes, and if anyone needed help with payments, contracts, or transfers, he was the go-to person. People often praised him for fixing mistakes and quickly solving money problems. He played a major role in handling the company's finances and oversaw payments sent to creators. Whether people got paid on time ultimately came down to him. What no one knew was that behind this friendly and helpful front, Dennis was stealing millions of dollars from the company to fund his gambling addiction.

Over the years, Dennis stole about $22 million. He was eventually caught by the FBI and sentenced to more than six years in prison. The company shut down the same year, leaving thousands of creators without representation. For us, it was especially shocking because we had once personally relied on Dennis to fix a payment issue with a $13,000 check. He was promptly responsive, even sending screenshots to prove the wire transfer. We sent him a thank-you gift, not realizing we were dealing with someone who was actively stealing from the company.

The payment took days to actually show up, and we eventually received a double payment by mistake. Dennis told us not to worry and said he would deduct it the next month. Looking back, we wonder if this kind of "error" may have been part of how he funneled money to himself. In a company with thousands of creators and poor internal oversight, something like this could have easily gone unnoticed for years.

The lesson is simple but important. When you trust someone else with your money, whether it's an agent, manager, or creator network, stay involved as much as possible! Never assume someone is trustworthy just because they appear to be kind and helpful. Keep clear records of all your financial transactions. Ask questions and follow up on anything that feels off. Scammers rely on being underestimated. They blend in, act charming, and hide behind busy systems or big company names. Dennis wasn't an outsider. He was a trusted employee, which made him even more dangerous.

In this industry, staying safe means staying alert and protecting yourself, even with the people you never expected to question.

Conclusion
Embrace the Future, Own Your Path

The world has changed, and whether we like it or not, there's no going back. Social media is woven into nearly every aspect of modern life, from the way we communicate to how we eat, shop, learn, and work. You can't hide from it. You can't pretend it doesn't exist. And really, why would you want to?

We live in a world where your ideas can travel across the globe with the click of a button and where success is no longer confined to traditional careers. The world has evolved. If you're reading this book, chances are you want to evolve with it.

There's still value in unplugging. There's nothing wrong with taking a walk, touching grass, or having a real conversation without a screen in sight. But if you want to move forward in today's world and build something that lasts, you'll need to understand how to navigate the digital space. That means learning how to create, how to show up consistently, and how to present yourself online in a way that aligns with your personal and professional goals. And yes, that might mean getting over the fear of looking silly.

As we conducted research for this book, the people we spoke with all had the same concern. They were afraid. Afraid of failure, afraid of being judged, afraid of not seeming cool. But here's the truth. Everyone who's ever accomplished something meaningful has looked a little cringy in the beginning. If no one ever risked looking awkward, we wouldn't have art or innovation.

You can't grow without stepping outside your comfort zone. So if you're holding back because you're scared of what people might say, it's time to let that go. Success on social media is not linear. Some weeks, everything clicks. Your views are up, brands are reaching out, and your audience is growing. Other weeks, it feels like no one is watching and nothing is working. That's normal. What matters most is how you respond. Can you pivot when something flops? Can you restructure when things stall? Because while not everything is in your control, you have the power to adapt.

One thing that doesn't get talked about enough is the power of support. This isn't a solo journey. If you have just one person in your life who believes in you, lean on them. Maybe it's your mom, your partner, your best friend, your sibling, or your kid. Whoever it is, hold onto them. Celebrate your wins with them and let them be there for you when things get hard. This space can be lonely. Even though it often feels like you're on stage, creating content on social media can also be isolating. Having even one person who understands what you're trying to do makes all the difference. For us, that person was each other.

We also want to be honest about the realities of building a brand. It is competitive. The barrier to entry is low, and that means there are a lot of people vying for attention. And make no mistake, attention is the new currency of the digital age. It can be even more valuable than money. Where attention goes, power, opportunity, and growth follow.

But here's the thing. Most people think "great content" is the secret. And while content does matter, it's not the whole picture. Great content is subjective. It doesn't have to be filmed with expensive gear or edited to perfection. Great content can be shot on your phone in your car, in one take, with no makeup and no script. It's about connection, clarity, and, of course, strategy.

However, don't fall into the trap of thinking there's nothing left to learn. We're here to say, with love, that almost everyone's content can be improved. The best creators are always evolving.

You want to create. You want to grow. You want to share something with the world. And you absolutely can. There is room for you. Not just to exist online, but to thrive.

This world favors the bold, the curious, and the ones who are willing to try and keep going even when it's hard. You don't have to have it all figured out. You just have to start. The rest will come.

So go out there and create something. Show up. Be brave. Stay curious. Stay kind. Keep learning. Above all, remember that what you build today could change your life tomorrow.

You've got this.

Acknowledgments

From the Authors

First and foremost, a huge and heartfelt thank-you to our incredible literary agent, **Rachel Beck at Liza Dawson Associates** and the entire Liza Dawson team. We are so grateful for your guidance and support throughout this process. Thank you for believing in us and in our vision, and for helping us bring our dream to life. It still feels surreal.

Our deepest gratitude to our wonderful publishing team at **BenBella Books**. Above all, thank you to our exquisite editor, **Victoria Carmody**, for shaping our work into what it is today. Your edits made this book infinitely better.

Thank you as well to our initial editor, **Claire Schulz**, for reading the earliest drafts of this project and offering such thoughtful feedback.

A special thank-you to **Sarah Avinger** for designing our beautiful cover, and to **Glenn Yeffeth, Madeline Grigg, Alicia Kania, Clara Tamez, Monica Lowry**, and **Anthony LaSasso** for your support along the way.

We are endlessly grateful to each of you.

From Shanna

When I was little, every time someone asked me what I wanted to be when I grew up, my answer was always the same: A writer. Even at seven years old, I never hesitated. As I grew, I became a storyteller on social media and a visual artist. Somehow, all the winding paths of my life led me right back here, to writing.

I am writing this while putting my sixteen-month-old daughter to bed. She will be two years old by the time this book reaches shelves. I became a mother and wrote this book at the same time, caring for a newborn as the pages came together. My daughter was barely two months old when we signed the contract.

Writing this book during my baby's first year was no small feat. It was built in nap times, babysitter hours, and late evenings (once she finally slept through the night).

During this journey, something remarkable happened. Many of the women in my agency and publishing world also become mothers, got pregnant, or went on maternity leave, stepping into this new chapter of life alongside me. It was a powerful reminder of what mothers are capable of and how we can carry creation in more ways than one.

So thank you to my baby girl, my brilliant, mischievous little elf, for making me a creator in a new and incredible way. You cannot talk yet, but your happy squeaks, which remind me of Pokémon sounds, are the soundtrack of this season of my life. And thank you to my husband, whose love brings color to every page of my world.

From Marissa

There's a famous saying in martial arts: a black belt is just a white belt who never quit. I started my martial arts journey over half a decade ago, and I can still remember the day I put on my very first pair of gloves. I was a fish out of water, flailing the entire time at something completely foreign to me. Looking back years later as an almost black belt who's survived injuries, broken bones, and more punches to the face than I could ever count, I can say that growing on social media and writing a book are very similar to practicing martial arts. They all take years of hard work, slowly chipping away at a dream that oftentimes, only you can see. There are days when you want to give up or throw in the towel, and moments when you feel like no one is in your corner. It's important that you keep going anyway.

To my incredible friends who make my life so rich and full, thank you for the coffee dates, HomeGoods shopping sprees, brunches, flea markets, dance classes, martial arts classes, trivia nights, movie nights, phone calls, and for always having my back. I'll always have yours.

To my amazing sister, who was the driving force behind this project and our social media journey in general, I couldn't have done any of this without your grit and determination. Thank you for guiding me through life and always being there for me. You're the best friend and sister anyone could ever ask for.

To the most beautiful, happy, bright, little lady on this planet, my niece. I hope one day you pick up this book and remember that you can accomplish anything in life.

To the most kick ass, best Sensei on the planet, Sensei Kian. Thank you for inspiring me with the martial art of Kapap Krav Maga and always training me. You are the Mr. Miyagi to my Karate Kid.

Lastly, to my orange fluffy cat Sushi, thank you for your endless kisses and cuddles, and plopping down into my arms as I was writing this book.

Index

About the Authors

Marissa Rachel is a Los Angeles–based Brazilian American content creator, host, and digital media entrepreneur best known as the creator of the wildly popular beauty, fashion, and lifestyle YouTube channel @MarissaRachel. With more than a quarter of a billion video views and a combined audience of over two million followers across platforms, Marissa has built a global community spanning millennials through Gen Z.

Her content blends fashion and beauty expertise with martial arts, pop culture, and sharp humor, establishing her as a distinctive voice in the creator economy. Marissa has hosted four seasons of the fashion competition television series *Ready, Set, Style*, which aired on the ITV2 Network in the United Kingdom.

A sought-after speaker and brand partner, Marissa has collaborated with some of the world's most recognizable companies, including Disney, Amazon, Twentieth Century Fox, Marvel, Victoria's Secret PINK, Olay, Always & Tampax, Toyota, Office Depot, and Procter & Gamble. She has spoken on the TEDx stage and at the United Nations General Assembly, USC School of Cinematic Arts, and industry panels hosted by Google and YouTube.

Shanna Lisa is a Brazilian American content creator, artist, and storyteller based in Los Angeles. She is the co-creator of the highly influential beauty, fashion, and lifestyle YouTube channel @MarissaRachel, which she runs alongside her sister. Together, their work has amassed over a quarter of a billion video views and a collective following of more than two million people across social platforms.

Known for her relatable voice and creative eye, Shanna connects with audiences through beauty and style inspiration, local travel and entertainment discoveries, and candid mom humor that reflects real life behind the scenes. Her work blends creativity, culture, and community.

Shanna has partnered with iconic global brands including Disney, Amazon, Twentieth Century Fox, Marvel, Always & Tampax, Toyota, Office Depot, Airheads Candy, and Procter & Gamble. She has also spoken on the TEDx stage, at the United Nations General Assembly, USC School of Cinematic Arts, and on panels with Google and YouTube.